Say I'm sorry to mother

G000061303

Carol Dix

Say I'm sorry to mother

Growing up in the sixties

Pan Original
Pan Books London and Sydney

for M. I., and C. B.

First published 1978 by Pan Books Ltd,
Cavaye Place, London SW10 9PG
© Carol Dix 1978
ISBN 0 330 25481 2
Printed in Great Britain by
Richard Clay (The Chaucer Press) Ltd, Bungay, Suffolk

Contents

'Dear dad, please send a crate of gin
and say I'm sorry to mother.'

Introduction

Say I'm Sorry to Mother stems from the girl I was in the summer of 1965. Then eighteen, just about to go up to University, I kept a notebook, jotting down some of the things that happened to us all, some of the best lines, biggest moments, and I scribbled then, 'This is the most important year of our lives.'

The idea began to bud when those same friends and I were twenty-five. I had a magazine article to write on what it felt like revisiting school. I asked one of the group to come with me so we could talk about it as we walked down that same driveway into the same classrooms.

By the time we were twenty-eight, I was a journalist and that same friend was doing her own thing. We started to meet in the pub opposite the British Museum one evening a week to talk about ideas, feelings, our own work.

I think it was her original idea, and me who put it into motion. Wherever the book came from, we feel wonder at the fact that our very real friendship, that has progressed from the age of eleven, through the years, over the ups and downs, is now the subject matter of a book. How extraordinary, we say, quite modestly. But then we have always been interested in our own history – because through it we read the story of a generation. We feel that any young woman in her early thirties, or late twenties, will relate, will read about herself, in the stories of our lives.

The four of us are real people – I have just fictionalized names because we are not so brave as to expose ourselves totally in public. We all met in the first year at grammar school, back in 1958. We went through school as a group, went on to different universities.

In a strange way we followed each other about – moving to different places – until, by our late twenties, we were all living in London, single, some in a career, others out, some with men, others on and off. The need to write the book came from the fact we were nearing thirty, which proved to be more of a crisis point than any of us dared imagine.

What we had to find out was not only why we were there, living that kind of life, but how we had got there. The end of the book may strike you as being sad or depressing. There we all are, after our brave beginnings, thirty, sounding frightened and possibly bitter that we are on our own. I have to say that we can laugh at it now because, even as I write this a year later, things have eased for each of us. We feel happier, more secure in ourselves. But the reality had to be faced and that was painful.

The idea of the book is to say, for the first time, what it felt like to be a girl, a woman, in the late 50s, 60s and early 70s.

We were a specific generation. We were born immediately after the War into a changed society, changing faster as we grew up. We were given a lot of freedom that even elder sisters by three or four years did not have. We grew up alongside major events like the beginnings of the Beatles, the mini-skirt, the Pill, Bob Dylan, flower-power, Germaine Greer, alternative life-styles, dropping out, drugs, legal abortion.

We were told, even if in whispered voices, that we could do anything we wanted. The world was there for us to take for ourselves, and our lives were open canvases on which we could paint a picture of our own choosing.

I am not the first to say that freedom can be a hard mate. Freedom is fun, but scary. Now, when I look back to try to do the accounts, I realize there were no ruled margins, no blue lines to run across, no neat formulae for how our lives should be run.

That was where the idea began. It was easy to plan out. I knew what sort of lives we had led. I just had to write it. But that was where the next crisis began.

Who was *I* to be writing this book? I had not led a particularly exciting life, or a different one. Nothing I'd done was any worse, or more salacious, or more daring, than any other girl. Who on earth would want to read about the life of an ordinary girl from a middle of the road, provincial background?

There was no anger, no tragic incest, rape at twelve, mother hatred, resentment at being conditioned by men. None of it seemed to shout and scream in the voice that women had adopted by the early 70s. I didn't follow party-line feminism. I didn't even feel particularly conditioned into being a female.

I went to the newspaper library to do some research. I ran

8

through all the top twenties, all the books, films and fashions. I followed the stories of my favourite film stars, Liz Taylor and Marilyn Monroe; of the models; the ideas of the time. I'll never forget the day I reached 6 August, 1962 and, knowing what was coming next, but not wanting to admit it, I burst into tears as I saw the banner headline MARILYN IS DEAD.

As a child of my generation, I have grown up through the Women's Movement. As I became a young woman, people were writing and talking about the mistakes women had made, about the cruel deception played on them by men, and I had believed it, taken it to heart. But I was never fully convinced by it all. Somewhere, at the back of my mind, I felt it was going to be impossible to throw out all that other side of female life, to turn immediately the other way. I knew I understood what all girls must feel.

I wrote it down that afternoon, in the newspaper library, 'I know why Norma Jean wanted to be a movie star. So probably do most of the girls of my age. Norma Jean wanted to be a movie star because people told her how pretty she was, and she wanted to believe it. She wanted to be up there on the giant mirror and have everyone gaze at her face, and at her self. She wanted everyone to love her, just as she loved herself when she looked in the mirror. I know I grew up wanting to be a princess, to be adored and put up on a pedestal, and at the same time hating myself for it. It's complicated being a girl, or a woman.' And that won't change.

I asked my group of friends if they would help me with the book. Lovingly, unsuspiciously, uncompetitively, they said they would. We met on those dark, wintry nights, and talked as we have always talked, honestly and intimately, but this time a tape recorder was taking it all down. They were long, unwieldy conversations, except I was prompting them to dig deep, and tell me what they really felt and thought at various times in their lives.

Because we know each other so well, we have been honest. We have revealed things to each other never said before. And I know how valuable the revelations will be to other women. It is is hard to say these things.

I could never in my life as a journalist have interviewed

9

strangers, or women of a newer acquaintance, and had them reveal such intimate details. While we were doing the tapes, I think we were all aware that this was important. We had a heavy time of it. It's not a laugh to drag yourself into the mind of the fifteen- or seventeen-year-old you. We began to see how much we had changed, or how much we were the same person developed further.

I then took this jumble of material, the notes on cards from the newspaper research and the sheets of transcribed tape, away with me to the country and sat with it spread all over the table and the form of this book evolved before my eyes.

I never knew I was going to write it this way. I tried writing it more as the journalist, but it came out on the dull and pompous side. I kept thinking: 'I shouldn't have embarked on this; it should be a novel, in the modern confessional style.' But then that would not have been as true. A novel would have meant the story of my friends' lives, but all through the filter of my own eyes. As it is, you have their stories, without my authorial power to juggle and make them fit a preconceived pattern. They've checked their characters and told me when I got them wrong.

There is no moral, resounding ending that makes you feel 'Oh yes, that's how it should have been.' There is no concern with dramatic outline, and telling a story. The only concern is to get across very honest, intimate revelations about how a few girls felt about their lives and responded to certain changes, freedoms, in the world around them.

They have not said, 'Of course I followed my career and did not care about men,' because that is the political tone of today. They have laughed at themselves and admitted, 'I tried to be good and follow the idea of building up my own life, but really all I was doing was trying desperately to get such and such a boy interested in me, or to find the right man.' They have not ended up saying, 'Of course it's a better world we live in now, because women can do their own thing.' They are saying, 'I *feel* as if I know what I'm about, but sometimes I have terrible doubts. Maybe we all just went wrong, and what we should have done was marry at twenty-one, had kids and a nice traditional way of life.'

But why the title? I could theorize and say that we have to say we're sorry to our parents at some point. We really do. We have done things that upset them, and if they read about them now, they will still be upset. When I was working on the book that same summer, I began to realize the enormity of what I'd done. This would actually appear in print, and people would see it and say 'Oh, that's your daughter is it?' How embarrassed my parents would feel. I realized I had to say I was sorry again, for putting them through this further excess.

Why couldn't I just keep quiet, and be a decent, honest, hard-working girl? That's all they wanted from me. Nice girl, nice husband, nice children, maybe a bit of a job, but nothing too exceptional. Know your place, be the kind of good woman people talk about after she's gone. And here I was about to be an embarrassment again. So I wrote them a letter, explaining how I could say I was sorry, but it wasn't going to stop me writing what I wanted to say, any more than I ever stopped doing what I wanted to do in my youth – just for their sakes. They'll understand. They always have done.

But that is all theory. The title comes from a joke I remember from that eighteen-year-old summer. One of those flip, rather cynical, crass lines only young girls, who are sounding more bold than they really feel, can come out with. The line was crucial: there we were, setting off, hungry for life, in the big wide world, out to grab all we could get, and yet our lust was tarnished with fear. It was pre-Pill, pre-legal abortion days, and we knew the very real fears. 'Dear dad,' the joke letter ran, 'please send a crate of gin and say I'm sorry to mother.'

I know this book is important. It is the first time such conversations, that go on between girl friends and women friends, have ever appeared in print. It's all new, and for the first time. Whenever they go on about the 50s and 60s, it is always about the boys, and what they were up to. Girls appear as rather used and sad little figures, in their stick-out petticoats, white cardigans, and beehive hairdos. They get laid, they get pregnant, they get abused. But no-one has ever written before what it was like to be *that* girl.

Girls didn't feel they were being used and abused. Those girls weren't hanging around the fairgrounds and dance halls, as part of some masochistic charade. They were living *their* lives, wanting to be there, getting their fun and thrills. The reasons why, you'll read about in the book. But it is time somebody came out and said, 'Yes, we enjoyed it. We had fun in our lives. It may have been difficult, it may have been a struggle in places, but it's our story, and they can't take that away from us.'

1 Eve's shame

It happens when you are about ten. You first grow some under-arm hair, a fine sprouting of fair fuzz. No-one mentions it. Your mother keeps quiet and you look at it secretly and with some excitement or shame. Then, within a few months, there is a definite swelling in the breasts, little mounds are growing outward. You don't caress your new body wonderingly and lovingly. After all you have no idea what all this womanhood thing is, nor any desire to know. You wish it would all go away, and leave you in peace. Worse is when pubic hair starts to grow. It's the first time you've even noticed down there. You know nothing about sexual organs except that babies come out from there and somehow a seed from a daddy gets into a mummy that way. If you were like me, you did not explore or do any of those wild things girls are advised to do now. You did not even question. All I had done was notice the strange layers of pink flesh on baby girls when they trotted happily around naked. The pink leaves, one over the other, and the gap between. Perhaps thought had taken sub-conscious root.

The trouble with gender when it does hit, is that it hits hard. One summer holiday, I brought my towel and nightie along to the bathroom in my aunt's house as usual, to be turned away rather embarrassedly by the adult women. They would not say why they looked embarrassed, except that I was too old now, at ten, to share the bath with my boy cousin. It was one of the nastiest days of my life. I knew there was something different about me, that he would stare and probably make comments, but somehow I'd prepared myself for that. I was ready to take that embarrassment and then carry on as normal. He would get used to the fact I had hair and little breasts. My aunt and mother must have been embarrassed because they had expected me to read a sexual meaning into my changing body. They expected me to see myself as one of the women. But I really didn't. I felt terrible, dragged away from my friends, shut away like an unclean thing. And from that moment I felt distinctly uncomfortable with my new body.

But a girl like me was completely unconscious of what being a girl meant. That same year, playing with a young boy in his sister's bedroom, we came across a brown paper bag in the wardrobe with something inside. It was me who opened it and found these funny white things, made of cotton wool and paper. They were long, thin, crescent-shaped, with loops at the ends, and had blood on them, dried-out blood. In the heat of that summer day, he and I passed them between us, staring at the blood, at the way they had been pressed into a curved half-moon shape, and we tried to work out what they were. We guessed they must be something she was ashamed of, because they were hidden away. The worst thing we could think of was that she had shaved her underarms and used them as bandages. That same summer I was into dirty jokes and delighted in horrifying that boy with all those knicker wetting giggles over 'it' and number ones and twos. A year later though, I can remember feeling embarrassed playing with my cousins when we were skipping and my breasts, now getting more pronounced and independent of my chest, bounced up and down. The little girls laughed at me. I was different now. Our games were never the same again. Breasts bouncing up and down, being fairly uncomfortable, tell the young girl her behaviour has to change, that she cannot have the same freedom as younger girls and boys. Soon I didn't want to play the same sort of games any more.

When I was eleven I went with the other girls who had passed the 11 Plus to the girls' grammar school in Burton-on-Trent. Burton was an ordinary, rather grey and unattractive industrial town. In the mid-50s, a pall of brewing smells hung over it. An acrid smell of hops and malt. The dirty River Trent ran through the middle of the town and the most vivid picture it leaves is of the wide grey bridge over the river along which long queues of girls in school uniform idled to and from school. In our first year at that grammar school I met up with Georgina, Heather and Polly and we are still friends. At that age there were other girls who made up the gang, like Mag, Ellie and Pattie. But they've gone their separate ways now.

Polly was in many ways the leader. Little and romantic looking, with frizzy hair and large wide eyes, she had a natural confidence that made her brave. She was a dreamer who loved to draw pictures. Heather was quieter and more introverted, but she had a tough streak under it. She was always drawing too. Georgina was chattery, nervous and bookish. Mag was the brave, tarty one, Ellie very much the artistic dreamer, and Pattie needed to feed off the sense of adventure in the others.

There were thirty girls in each class, and three classes in each year at that school. Thirty aspiring, evolving, emerging young women – and what an incredible amount of energy was thrown up between them. There were several different groups. The sophisticated group led the way at first. They had arrived at school already going steady. They all lived in one area of town and somehow all had achieved the same status – steady boy-friends. They used to whisper at eleven and twelve about 'going all the way' and by fifteen I'm sure they had. They had their boyfriends and their snogging sessions. There wasn't much communication between us. They sat at the back, in the right hand corner and dominated the atmosphere with their cynical commentary.

There were the soft ones next, who wanted boyfriends, but not for the sex status so much as with the serious idea of getting married as soon as possible. There were the ones we called the 'science' girls, who incredibly went towards physics, maths and chemistry. They seemed rather asexual.

Then there was our group. To be a member of that you had to have some or all of these dreams. You had to want to get out, out of Burton, out of small town hopes and desires. That's why the going-steady group weren't envied by us. You had to be interested in the theatre, the arts, cinema, and the pop world. You had to be interested in rockers, teds, beats and any male who was in some way nasty, earthy, wild and not at all like those sexually immature grammar-school boys down the road. You had to yearn to look sultry, sexy, and be like a rocker yourself. You had to want to swear and sound bolder than you were, to be intellectually superior to most of the people you knew and to want to live 'dangerously'.

HEATHER I remember getting to know Polly. We were in the first form of grammar school. I knew I wasn't one of the lot who lived for boys even then at eleven or twelve. I fantasized about men like film stars and wrote fan letters to Dirk Bogarde. But Polly was a funny little thing even then. She didn't have a mother and I'd been told by my mother to be friendly towards her. I made an effort and we just clicked. We both liked dressing up and we used to spend the weekend with one another. We had the most fantastic dressing-up clothes – all our aunts' clothes that I wish I had now. We'd stuff the busts of the dresses with paper. We lived in such a fantasy world then. Saturdays were absolutely marvellous. In the morning, we went down to the library. Books were so important, and the rest of the time we acted out our fantasy worlds. It was with her that I first started writing and drawing. I do realize that we would have been really lost if we hadn't been kindred spirits. Polly was a natural bohemian even then because she was totally unselfconscious.

POLLY I always thought I was a happy little girl. It's only now I realize that I wasn't most of the time. I don't remember being actively unhappy but I think a lot of the time I must have been. My immediate impression of myself as a little girl is of being rather pouty, bad-tempered, a bit timid, sulky and miserable. My dad used to call me 'piggy lip' because I pouted so much. I was the youngest of four and maybe I didn't get the attention I wanted – which is probably why I reverted to a fantasy world. It was all to do with fantasy men and movie stars, and it began at around five for me.

HEATHER My childhood was complicated by one very bad experience. I was a very extroverted, self-confident little girl until school. I was the youngest of four too and the apple of my mother's eye. Then I went to a convent school. I was the only Protestant in a Catholic convent and the nuns picked on me. They used to criticize me for everything I did and make an example of me in front of the others by calling me a heathen Protestant. I think they resented me for being an individual. It got so that I became really embarrassed to make a show of myself at all. I remember I used to wet my knickers because I didn't dare put my hand up to ask to go to the toilet, and then to make things worse I'd have to go home wearing a nun's knickers.

POLLY Before I got to grammar school, I remember my brother and I grew up together in the country, though we didn't actually play together. He had his gang of boys and I had my girlfriends.

He spent most of his time over the fields learning about nature. And I spent most of my time over the fields in total fantasy! We were story-tellers. My first friend was Sue. There was George (a girl) too. We used to keep the story going for ages: playing at being chased by bandits. We acted it all out. I did the same at school with fairy stories. We were always being boys having adventures rather like the Famous Five.

I don't think little boys had any more adventures than us. They were more practical that's all, making dams and stuff. With Sue and George, I dressed up. I had a huge dressing-up box of wonderful clothes. I wish I'd never thrown them away. I used to march off to jumble sales to buy them – a long blue velvet dress for 3d – it was my pride and joy. We dressed up as ladies, very splendid in long dresses. It was all up in our top attic, very dusty and out of bounds really.

I was a bit of a tomboy and a bit of a little girl. I had shorts and T-shirts and also some lovely little smocked dresses. I don't recollect having much say in what I wore till I was thirteen or fourteen, by which time it was battles over ankle socks and bras.

But my fantasy life started, I'm sure, from the feeling that nothing I'd ever done was really encouraged. I wasn't even allowed to think I was pretty. I was told by my sister that when I was very young I was very sweet with long ringlets down to my waist and someone once said to me 'Oh, isn't she pretty, what a pretty little thing' and I said 'Yes, I am rather beautiful, aren't I' in a sweet little voice. It must have been a very early little buzz that said 'I'm all right.' But it was immediately slapped down by my parents as vanity. I was not allowed to be anything creative or individualistic, or unusual. So I resorted to fantasy. Inside I was saying 'One day I'll show you I am extraordinary really.' I always envied Georgina at school, because she believed in herself. Utterly.

GEORGINA I don't know if I ever felt like a little girl. I wasn't a tomboy – I was far too scared. But I always felt like a stranger in my own shoes. I was the adored baby girl of my father, and he loves women, so I got all his adoration. I was 'his baby'. I had pretty silvery hair and I presume I was sweet, though my earliest memories are of prickling against being seen as sweet. I don't remember my girlfriends till I was about ten. I suppose because

I didn't have any stable ones. By then, when we were living in a big house, I made friends with a girl at the junior school. I was very possessive. I had one friend I adored, and I expected the same in return. She was little and cute to my tall lankiness. I'd decided I was ugly. I was always thin, and had rather greasy hair. I didn't feel attractive to boys and I hated myself for it. I remember playing 'kiss chase' in the school yard and, when I was caught, I'd say to the boy: 'It's all right, you don't have to kiss me.' I became bookish as a way out.

HEATHER I didn't entertain any illusions about boys at all. I had my brothers who used to torture me, and at junior school boys had been the people you had to dance with and who crushed your hand. You know – the 'puppy-dogs' tails' syndrome. Apart from Jen, my artist-type friend at that age, my gang of girls included Annette, who was the daughter of a divorcée and Nan, who was blonde, working-class and had already developed breasts. I remember the others used to look at me with pity and asked me once if there was barrenness in my family! I was a very late developer and had no breasts at all at ten or eleven. We got Annette to ask her mother if she fucked to have her! We knew the word but not what it meant.

GEORGINA My first hint of my latent sexuality only came when I was walking with a girlfriend over the fields in front of our house in Burton. The fields spread for a good mile between two main roads. They're gone now, of course, under a council estate. But then they were wild, untamed, with cows that frightened me, cow-pats, ponds and streams. She and I were meandering along when we were ambushed by four small boys who I recognized as a family of brothers from a corner house nearby. They were an aggressive looking lot who had scared me several times. They ambushed us in earnest and lifted up our skirts to look at our knickers, and made rude comments which I didn't understand then.

This I do remember: they put their hands down our jumpers and I felt a tingling sensation in my breasts. I recognized it as excitement, as something enjoyable. I felt a bit ashamed of it, as obviously it had been done in a rather foul, grabbing way. My friend and I were both shocked but we didn't talk about it between ourselves. Breasts had become something of an obsession with me. I was dying to see someone's but everyone I knew kept theirs well hidden. One night, I nearly crept into my sister's bedroom, imagining I would pull the covers back, lift up her nightie, and take a quick look. I tried to fit the pieces together and asked her once if a girl at school, called Valerie, who already had big breasts, was pregnant. No – it did not mean that – but no more was I told.

POLLY Mine began with an early kiss, when I was eight, from my brother's friend who must have been eleven. We were playing in the bales of hay, and he said 'Have you ever had a French kiss?' and I said 'No.' I got the 'mouth open and tongue' bit. I remember a tingle down my spine and I actually thought 'This is nice.' I had crushes on schoolboys in those days. One of them used to bring me a rose every Friday. That was the romantic thing, not sex. I think I still have an ideal image somewhere. It's still romantic. I lived on romantic fantasy as a teenager.

Oh, yes, but I also had a sexual experience when I was three or four, more of an interfering-with. I was on some bombsite – it's a terribly vague memory – with my little cousin, picking flowers. This man came up to me, to pick flowers for me, then he put his fingers in my knickers, picking flowers with the other hand, saying 'Here you are, little girl.' I was in that squatting position, completely absorbed in what I was doing. I remember thinking 'I don't think you should be doing this.' I definitely did not leap up and run away. There was a feeling somehow, because he was a grown-up and a man, of 'I've got to put up with this.' I didn't even start to cry because he wasn't my daddy, he was a complete stranger. It didn't bother me, till years later I remembered it and told my brother.

GEORGINA My mother let me into the Big Secret by giving me a little book one day when I was eleven. It was in a brown envelope and it came, I noticed, from *Woman*, the magazine she read. Intriguing. She told me to read it and then come and ask her anything I did not understand. The trouble was I did not understand a word of it. What I read was all about ashes: the body of a woman cleaning out its own ashes once a month, and not to be frightened by it as it was a purifying process. I failed to see the word 'blood' because I'd already got the image of ashes – as we cleaned the grate out every day – lodged firmly in my mind. So

I had to ask my mother, who was clearly upset. She told me about periods. She explained that you lose blood once a month, that it starts in adolescent girls any time from eleven to fourteen. That I would probably start quite early as all the women in her family had done. She showed me a packet of sanitary towels and a belt – one of those horrid pink cotton and satin ones, and said next time we went into town we would get me one, so I'd be all ready. But I was still nowhere near prepared for the real shock of it. A young girl cannot really grasp that she is going to lose blood out of the gap between her legs, once a month, for the foreseeable future. And that she's not to worry about it either!

We were on holiday, by the sea, the summer I was nearly twelve. It was a typical English seaside holiday; cold, wet, blustery and hardly tempting to go in the water. I began to wonder what was going on when I had brown stains in my knickers for several days. I thought I must have diarrhoea. Then it happened – the reddish brown flow. My mother saw it, my sister came to look. They rushed round finding me my belt and first sanitary towel. They were putting them on me with an air of excitement. But I felt like a young horse that has had its foot bandaged and cannot run around and play any more. Surely this wasn't going to happen every month for the rest of my life? It didn't seem possible that something so clumsy could go on month in, month out. It made your life feel regularized. They said I'd better not go in the sea again that holiday. I cried. I hated the sea really.

My father kept his distance. There was no place for a man in these rituals. But I ran and caught up with him, secretly saying 'Let me walk with you, I don't want to be part of that.' It was the most disappointing day – ever. It is no wonder girls grow up and mature more quickly than boys. We learn one of life's shitty lessons very early on. That any freedom you take will be countered with a measure that stops or affects it.

When you see blood coming out of you, you know it is something girls have that boys don't. You immediately internalize, put your thoughts right back up that vaginal gap, back up inside you, into your own body and feelings.

HEATHER I didn't come on till I was fourteen. By then, of course, I knew all about it as everyone at school talked about it. I worried in case mine never came. When it did, I was really proud and felt a sense of status. My mother had given me one of those brown-covered books too and said 'I suppose you know all about it.' I told her I did, but really I felt contempt that she could not tell me herself. She must have bought me my first sanitary towel and belt because I don't remember buying it.

POLLY As my mother was dead, my dad asked my sister to get me through adolescence. Unfortunately she never told me anything. One day, when she was home from university, she asked me to get her an ST out of a drawer. Of course I knew where they were. I'd snooped around and found them ages before. She asked me then if I knew all about it and I said yes, though I didn't really. I think she was a bit embarrassed to say much and I was too embarrassed to say I didn't know! So my confidence put her off. She told me it would probably begin soon and I should be prepared. That's all. She left me to buy my first packet of sanitary towels and belt, which was awful. For weeks, I hovered round that chemist's shop waiting to see if the man would go off the counter. I'd go in, chicken out and buy something else. In the end, Heather and I were together at her house, dressing up. I'd put on a black swimsuit when we both noticed this blood. She had one towel which her mother had given her, so I borrowed it. A year later, when she came on for the first time, she whispered across to me in school if she could have it back!

GEORGINA After the first trauma or shock, I don't think girls continue to hate the world, or God, or their mother, for the fact they menstruate – that was the word for it then, wasn't it, not periods? But the whole thing was extremely, excessively, embarrassing. When we got to grammar school there was the inevitable older girl who made sure we all knew about it. At twelve, it was your one main obsession. She went round the form asking who had come on and who not. But it was all very well for her to be brave, we had our private terrors to go through. In our day we were more embarrassed by periods than anything else. It would have been much easier if we could have discussed it with each other.

In the days of the sanitary towel, which you carried to school at the bottom of your satchel in a crumpled brown paper bag so it got squashed beneath homework and littered with pencil shavings and ink stains, you were instructed to burn them in the incinerator rather than flush them away. There can be no more irrational and silly fear than waiting in the toilet cubicle till the last voice has gone so I could dash out and tip the dreaded thing into the incinerator when no-one was looking. And those awful times at assembly when the headmistress would say again, 'Girls are not to put STs down the toilets as they clog up the drains and the maintenance man has to clear them out.' Oh, God, the images that conjured up as I secretly blushed knowing it was mine he had found.

POLLY I never used school incinerators. I could not bring myself to. I'd take them home again in my satchel, collect up about twelve old ones – Oh hell, what a memory! – in a drawer in my bedroom and wait for the one evening when my father was out and the fire was lit, so I could get them all burned and the smell gone before he came back. For those two years at school, before I came on, me and Sue used to be fascinated by the bins, incinerator, and brown paper bags made by Southalls. We were never sure what they were for.

GEORGINA I used to collect them at home too, and burn them in the boiler on a Saturday morning. They gave off a fish-glue kind of smell which seemed to fill the house and I'd pray my father wouldn't come home and ask what the smell was. Also I'm afraid those school incinerators got stuck in my mind with the first things I learned about Jews in the concentration camps. I was never able to disassociate the smells.

POLLY We had terrible problems with soaking through sanitary towels, never knowing whether putting two on at once showed, never daring to ask for Lilia's or Dr White's at the chemists.

GEORGINA One of the first lousy tricks we learned was that, although we were allowed to be at the grammar school, to be as clever as the boys, try for the same exams, the exam system was cleverly devised by men for men with boys in mind. For girls who had heavy periods on exam day, there was no way to get through the whole three hours without some disaster. Even wearing two towels was not enough and no one let you go out to change one. Exams were always in summer and the bright red patch at the back showed up if you went through.

POLLY And you probably got a stomach ache too. There is only one thing you want to do when you have a stomach ache, and that is curl up into yourself or sit hugging the radiator. That's when girls learn to sit around chatting, gossiping, doing nothing. You don't feel like doing anything, particularly being mentally active. The mind switches off, away from the outside world, and vanishes into the inner world.

GEORGINA Periods always seemed to come on damp, grey days when your inner feelings expressed the outer day. I soon began to see that my emotions were master of my body. If I had exams coming up and my periods were following neatly in my diary – every month three days late or something – then I could be sure that once it got wind of the exams coming up it'd change the pattern and come five or eight days late, so I'd coincide beautifully slap, bang, there at the beginning of the exams. If I was going on holiday and desperately hoped it would come on time and be over with, it would of course delay itself and say 'hello' the day I went away. That's when I learned that emotions are much stronger than reason – a lesson men can take years to learn.

At the same time, passions were beginning to work in other mysterious ways. I would be gripped by people kissing on television. It was a fascination linked with horror. I wondered for many years whether, to be kissed, the women had to put her arms up loosely round the man's neck and accept his head coming down on hers while she leaned backwards. It seemed, even with no experience, a rather cool pose for the woman. Not much grip or passion from her in a Hollywood kiss. My own dreams at that stage were always of a couple kissing or rolling around in the grass and as I got nearer they of course disappeared. I didn't know what else they should be doing, so I couldn't have got any nearer.

HEATHER I just lived in a fantasy world of film stars like Dirk Bogarde till I was fifteen. I wasn't very pretty. Then I started going with Mag to dances. I went to one dance in the summer – a vivid memory of all the girls crowded into one room, peering into the same mirror, and tarting themselves up. Anyway, at this dance I met the first boy I ever kissed. All I knew was that I was determined he wouldn't find out he was the first person. Afterwards, he said 'Where did you learn to kiss like that?' and

23

instead of saying 'Actually in bed, on my pillow' (I used to practise what I'd seen on TV), I said 'Oh, I couldn't tell you.'

POLLY I'd already learned what a kiss was at eight. Then, when I was about thirteen, I had a crush on another of my brother's friends. At fourteen it was finally reciprocated. He was seventeen, dark-haired and dark-eyed – all that archetypal number I loved. Eventually he came into my room one night and kissed me. I have this image of him walking across my room and I thought 'Oh, no, I can't bear it.' I didn't actually want it. Sexually, at that time, I can't remember what I felt. I don't remember any of that writhing on sheets. I remember draping myself in the bathtowel, looking at my growing tits – what there was of them! And I explored myself, my fanny, and thought 'Oh, it's growing' – the lips were developing. Just curiosity. I was completely unaware of orgasm. All this bit about little girls bringing each other off. I didn't know it existed. I didn't know it existed till I was about eighteen, let alone experience it.

GEORGINA I didn't know the word for it, but I do remember feeling the urgency.

POLLY My whole teenage was taken up by going to the movies. Kissing was all right because they did it on films; it was beautiful and romantic and it all involved looking across crowded rooms and eyes meeting. It was actually nothing to do with cunts and pricks and all that body stuff. By the time I got to sixteen, the endless actors and film stars I had crushes on would get as far, in my fantasies, as the loving and the meeting, but I used to block the getting into bed. Maybe I made us wait till we got married or at least till we were older. But he definitely would not do that kind of thing!

GEORGINA I had crushes on prefects at twelve. I really loved those older girls more, I think, as an emotional outlet than anything sexual. I never fantasized anything sexual. It was just loving and being loved. I mean hanging round school corridors waiting for my favourite to appear was only the same feeling a few years later when I was hanging round a street corner hoping my fantasy man would see me. All that shivering excitement. I once put my arms round a prefect in a moment of pure emotion and hugged her. Another one once sat close by me at a Girl Guide camp fire. I wrote stories about them, I think so I could live out the emotions of an older girl. But unfortunately I was so embarrassed by the stories that I burned them when I was fourteen.

At thirteen, I had a crush on Polly's elder brother. I'd get another friend to come with me for long bicycle rides. I loved those bike rides, shooting along country lanes, stopping to pick flowers, smelling the warm grass of summer, bathing our feet in a stream, riding with no hands, no feet, feeling the wind in our hair, and then freewheeling down into Polly's village, pedalling past their house, keeping my head down below window level in case he saw me. Once would have been all right. But every Saturday was a bit much and I'd have hated him and you to think I had a crush on him. I never saw him. But to be near is to love. I didn't want anything more, anyway, than the rush of excitement.

POLLY I wouldn't, you know. I was actually very proud that girls had crushes on him, because I was very proud of him.

GEORGINA But in bed at nights I did get really scared about myself that I would never have a boyfriend. I used to pray to my confidante, God, that I'd have a boyfriend by sixteen or that to put me out of my misery he'd let me go away and become a nun.

HEATHER I never had crushes on older girls at all. I was pretty repressed sexually till fifteen.

POLLY Nor me. My fantasy figures were boys from an early age. I remember the only books I wanted to read were about some Roman boys I'd seen on television. I thought Rufus or Marcus were so great. I loved the Famous Five too, but again it was for the boy characters. Later on it was those books like *He Went with Vasco da Gama*, or *Marco Polo*, or *Columbus*. They were all about seventeen-year-old lads stowing away on ships and I thought they were terrific. If the book involved danger, adventure in foreign parts, and was historical, with a young, attractive hero in it, I loved it. I think it was because I wanted to be the boy that I loved him so passionately.

But I'd started to create my own fantasy figures by then. Rainer Arden was the first one. I invented him and wrote a whole book about him as an early teenager. He was a Heathcliff kind of figure: thin-faced, dark-haired and dark-eyed; very beautiful in that sort of gypsy or primitive way – or very cultured and clever, and nobody would walk over him. He was very cool to the rest of the world, but not to me. He had that amazing manner that made people stop and stare. He wasn't weak, except with me as the woman he loved and trusted – he could afford to break down and weep in my arms. The rest of the time he was my protector, my knight in shining armour. He was a freak, of course – long-haired, probably an artist. I was never sure what he did, but he wore faded jeans. I wrote a thing about him in Folkestone, at seventeen, called 'The Hobo'.

GEORGINA When I did eventually get dragged along to the church youth club by Pattie, who rightly said I was in danger of becoming a swot and letting life pass me by, I soon learned one thing. I could kiss a boy and like the kissing, and want him to do more without my in any way liking him. I wore a skirt and a jumper rather than a blouse, because I knew it was easier for him to get his hands up without any of the fumbling bits that might have led to me having to say 'no'. I realized, I think, that I liked sex and if I could wait long enough I was really going to like it one day, a lot.

The battle for high heels and lipstick began then. After the regimen of Clarks' sensible sandals and bar-strapped shoes I felt truly wonderful in one-inch heels of dark blue leather, worn with a summer dress of bottle-green flower print on a white background, and my mother's bright red lipstick. Not graceful, elegant, but someone with a hint of what grown-up femaleness was going to be all about. There was something about that strutting, even on a one-inch heel, that said my body was up for grabs, right there at that moment. And, at long last, because I was tall for my age, it suddenly paid off. I looked sixteen or seventeen, not fourteen, and could pass myself off as being more experienced.

POLLY I was very much the little girl till twelve. But by thirteen, I was already beginning to pose. I was like a film star. I held myself like a little woman. I used to look through endless film manuals and could do the slutty, gamine, provocative little girl come-on, the BB in St Tropez. Or I could sit with my legs outstretched like Marilyn Monroe or the Françoise Sagan alluring young girl. Very sexually confident. But it was all a pose. The last prissy thing I remember doing was going to have a school photo taken and arguing terribly with my sister about wearing beads. They were white Poppitts and I insisted. She said they looked silly. But there I am in the photo very much the pretty little lady in her beads, smiling confidently out.

GEORGINA My sister was going out with boys by then. I used to be very impressed as they came to call. Nice clean looking young men, who I knew were never going to be my type, and I accepted even then that my type were (a) never going to be the ones who came to call and (b) were not going to be the kind I'd want my parents to see me with. I stayed in watching *Wagon Train* or *Bonanza*, and dreamed of Robert Horton (*Wagon Train*) or John Smith (*Laramie*) bringing their craggy cowboy bodies near mine as I sat with rollers in my hair in front of the fire, waiting for some mini-cowboy to come and find me in Burton-on-Trent. The only thing that did come near me were the whistles from lorry drivers or road menders as I walked down the road. That sexual comment did wonders for my confidence. To someone like me it was a real thrill.

ME Yes, when I read Ingrid Bengis's *Combat in the Erogenous Zone* not so long ago, where she describes that as part of mind-rape, I felt surely she can't be so dogmatic? When I was that age I had no confidence either and I needed those whistles. I like it even today. They can make you laugh. It's like you both enter the fantasy of what it would be like to have a casual fuck there and then. It's one of the freedoms we asked for anyway, to be able to come down off our pedestal where we were beyond sexuality, to be let down into the earthy jungle of equal sexual rights.

GEORGINA I learned about romance and emotion from books like historical novels and the ones by R. L. Delderfield and Dorothy Whipple. Or ones by Georgette Heyer and Frances Parkinson Keyes. It was Georgette Heyer and, at school, Jane Austen, who left me with the undying image of the strong male hero eventually riding in to carry me away. Though, somewhere at the back of my mind, despite the fact it didn't seem such a bad fate stuck, as I was, at home, I also knew that I would rather go and grab my own. The passive heroine-lying-in-waiting was not really going to be my scene.

The one book that gave me more than mild dreams was Nevil Shute's *A Town Like Alice*. I adored it, as it not only spelled out adventure in the Australian bush, which to me was the wildest place imaginable, but gave me my first big literary turn-on. There is a scene where the hero is with a young girl who is wearing just a sari-like piece of material wrapped round her. As he stands close up, the material drops, revealing her beautiful body. I longed for a scene like that in my own personal drama of life.

I had many a year to go, though, of sweaty nights, in lonely bedrooms, pacing up and down, not knowing what to do with the power of my feelings. That hot determined itch between your legs; the heat coming off your body; the closed-in, trapped, buried-alive feeling that, in early adolescence, is so hard to get rid of. That's the world of little girls, isn't it? In the evenings, I paraded up and down in front of long mirrors, taking off my nightie to look at myself. Stretching my naked body so I'd look more like a film star, a model, more desirable and beautiful. Caressing myself, and wanting someone to yearn for *me*. Wanting to drive a man crazy as I flexed a muscle or raised an eyebrow! It's the same now!

ME Yes, I tried reading some old diaries from those days. The kept-down, repressed, bottled-in feelings come out as listlessness, lethargy, despair and boredom. Oh, the boring days that passed into boring days! Nothing happened – school; hung around with so and so; rode home; nice tea; homework; watched TV. Another boring day. How I feel for that girl in me and wish I could rush back and help get her out of herself. It's at this point in my memories that I thank heavens I was born in this day and age. I cannot imagine that young girls of any other age in history suffered any less, felt any less of all that emergent sexuality, energy, hope and life-force. But they were never allowed to express it. The idea of being buried with all that still inside of you is the most terrible thought I have. That's where I say 'I'm sorry' to all the women in the past who were buried in the coffins of their own bodies. I'd have gone screaming mad if I hadn't been allowed to scream, and scream, and scream away some of that pent-up feeling. Luckily we were able to get out.

2 Life among the girls

It's funny to think now that girls' grammar-school education was relatively new even in our day. Burton's dated back to the 40s, but when I moved to Stratford-on-Avon that girls' grammar school had only been in existence for seven years. We asked – but what had girls done before that? Answer – not gone to grammar school. Yet we just accepted that such schools had always been there, because it was the only world we knew. There was nothing cosy, quaint, or 'you're only here to fill in time till you get married' about it either. We were at school to achieve, to go on and do great things, and to be as clever as possible. We noticed the sixth form and prefects getting their Oxford and Cambridge open scholarships (soon to be closed) and as we grew up so the size of the sixth forms grew too. We were at the beginning of the push to get as many boys and girls as possible to the redbrick universities. Boys and girls from working-class homes, with parents who had no academic aspirations, were now seeing themselves as potential university fodder. Girls, whose mothers had never imagined them as anything more than secretaries, were being caught up in the tide of enthusiasm.

We also wanted to have fun. We did not want to be like the prefects of two or three years ahead – they seemed drab and boring girls who had sacrificed their lives to getting on at school. We had this notion that it was possible for us to be clever, witty and bad, and still do well at school.

A certain style was being created as our school days went by. John Osborne had had his *Look Back in Anger* staged in the mid-50s, and now, by 1959, the term 'angry young man' was part of the language. We hoped we were the female equivalents of the angry young men.

The style was a bit of the rocker, a smattering of the Brigitte Bardot sulk, and naturalness, and a touch of the beat carelessness and amorality. Every school photograph of the time had every girl affecting the Bardot pout. We aspired to pass our exams while still hanging on to the image of the wild, free, wanton spirit. We hadn't read any of this in magazines at the time. Teen magazines only began with *Honey* in 1961, and I bought it religiously from the first issue, progressing from *Girl* and *Schoolfriend*, through odd snippets of my mother's *Daily Express* gossip columns, to the novels of people like Françoise Sagan.

We did our hair in the bouffant style, and stuck our skirts out with stiff petticoats; fought the teachers to wear stiletto heels at school, or at least black stockings. Mag, who was about five foot nothing, and wore three-inch heels that made her look like a whore, backcombed her hair up a good four inches at the front.

She was the one who gave the sexual advice, warning girls off the boys in town who only wanted to 'get it up yer'. We did not actually discuss sex in detail at that age – few of us knew what the details were, least of all Mag – but the aggressive talk was very exciting, rather than the whimsy hand-holding of some of the nice girls. We wanted experience, though the nearest most of us got to it in 1960 was the smuggled copies of *Lady Chatterley's Lover*, with their well-thumbed pages, that appeared after the Crown Court ruling.

The top ten was full of 'Magic Moments', Connie Francis's 'Who's Sorry Now', Laurie London's 'He's Got the Whole World in His Hands'. Later it was the Everleys, the Mudlarks' 'The Book of Love', Connie Francis's 'Stupid Cupid' and Elvis's 'King Creole'. There was the *6.5 Special*, with Jo Douglas and Jim Dale. But, more our style, and the name found inked over our satchels was Dirk Bogarde, *the* romantic hero for our kind of girl, in *The Wind Cannot Read*, and *The Singer Not the Song*.

The women's life-style we noticed, and wanted to copy, were bohemians like Sheelagh Delaney, and Françoise Sagan. *A Taste of Honey* came out in 1959, and soon there was *Bonjour Tristesse* and *A Certain Smile* to tell us how young girls really desired experience above all else. When Sarah Miles was in *Term of Trial* with Laurence Olivier in 1961, I remember being very excited by the film and her. I knew these lines by heart from the film: He: 'I want to help you as a teacher – as a father.' She: 'No. As a man. You like me as a man.' He: 'Please don't degrade yourself. I want to be your friend.' She (pulling him down on the bed): 'Then love me.'

The Twist had not started then. It was the tail end of the jiving era, but we did manage to smuggle into school Edith Piaf's

'Milord' and 'Je ne Regrette Rien' – we wanted a past over which we could have no regrets, too.

In the autumn of 1960, there was the Cuba crisis, though only a couple of us actually noticed it. Gagarin went up into space, Jack Kennedy became the new folk hero. There were race riots in the southern states of America and passive resistance became a talked-about phrase through Martin Luther King. The Ban the Bomb marches were given status by Vanessa Redgrave, John Osborne and Sheelagh Delaney sitting-in in Trafalgar Square.

GEORGINA My mother's highest aspiration for me was to become a politician's secretary because that meant I could work in the House of Commons. I somehow doubted it, but put myself down for that on the school forms at eleven.

HEATHER I'm sure we were lucky to have those spinster teachers though. At the time we laughed at them. Things they did or said were judged by us to be the reactions or actions of slightly crazed human beings, because they did not have men. Now I can see they knew things even our mothers did not. They wanted us to excel and knew that young girls have very bright minds which should not be wasted or tapped off in early marriage or mother-hood. I am glad, despite the lack of emotional education, that we went to a single sex school. Boys can't take over and you are not forever compared with them. For instance at junior school, which was mixed, my brother was always three years ahead of me. But I was always top of the class. My brother used to say to me 'Oh, when you get in the next form it's much harder then.' But I stayed at the top. That's until I had that conciliatory line from the teacher, 'Well, we do find girls do well *initially* but then at a certain point the boys take over'!

As for my mother's attitude, well, she and I always battled. She used to write to me at university and say 'I know you want to give it all up, get married and have babies.' That's what she thought women were for. She had to for her own sake. She was always the dunce at school, because she'd had to play mother to her own family. So the only thing she could do well was look after the house. For her, marriage was an escape from a world she couldn't cope with. But then, what was left of her life? Just an inner life, lived through looking after children.

GEORGINA It was only because of the grammar school we were

able to accept so easily our competitive urge, the need to succeed, the sheer fun of learning. Being the swotty type, I was extremely upset at fourteen though, when one of the other swotty types who had managed to drag a tame boy in tow for a year or so to cover for her social life, said to me scathingly and pityingly 'What is it like *never* to have had a boyfriend?'! But my pain wasn't as strong as a few months later when I cried, with another friend, because we only got 68 per cent in an English exam instead of being high up in the 70s or low 80s.

We loved English, we loved French – speaking it, reading it, listening to it, dreaming of French film stars, thinking of going to France. We hated physics with an aggressive boredom. They had refused to let us do biology beyond thirteen, because we were the clever ones being groomed for University, and it was thought that biology was a 'soft' subject. It's hardly surprising our emotional education was lacking. We had to drop all so-called soft, or female, subjects: art, needlework, cookery. We all had to get Latin 'O' Level for arts subjects at University.

But we were simply learning for the sheer lust of brainpower. Our minds were greedy, and still are. I'm sure girls are much cleverer than boys – they just get slowed down by their emotions from time to time. Between ourselves there was no shame in confessing we wanted to do well. Outside school you had to learn to cover it up.

HEATHER I did my hair in the bouffant style, putting rollers in the front so it stuck up like a beehive, backcombed fiercely and held by grips. Sleeping in rollers, the pins stuck in and made dents in my head. I never bothered to look at the back view in a mirror – it was too awful. The rocker image had really taken over. I wore stiff petticoats under my school summer dresses, layers of stiffened nylon net in pale blue, pink or yellow, with a straight cotton petticoat underneath to stop my legs getting too scratched. I wanted to wear stiletto heels but you couldn't in those days. We wore pointed toes if we could. The headmistress had to tell us not to wear the stiff petticoats, or at least not the hooped ones, as we could not all get in the school hall together.

By fourteen we were allowed to wear straight navy blue serge skirts, shirts with collars we could leave up, ties that went crooked. Our navy macs had their belts tied at the back. We stuck our berets on the back of our heads with grips, so they clung on under the beehive, and wore black stockings when we could get away with it! The sulky face went better with that outfit.

GEORGINA I remember reading *Lady Chatterley's Lover*. When *Lady C.* was cleared, the obligatory couple of copies circulated the school, with three pages turned down and well thumbed. We only wanted to read the 'thirteen acts in graphic detail', and of course got a terrible disappointment. I've re-read it recently and only wish now I'd given it more time then. It described so beautifully a woman's sexuality, her feelings and desires, her emotional confusions. Lawrence connects the bowels and the womb in her emotions. We could have made the connection as girls, because the hysteria that makes you want to 'wet yourself' is so similar to sexual feelings. 'If I laugh any more I really will wet my knickers,' you stutter out, and limping, jumping, hopping, try and get to the toilet in time!

Anyway, reading my old copy of *Lady C.*, I smiled to see the passage my teenage self had actually underlined. So much for teenage obsession with sex. What affected me was a paragraph about boredom:

And thus far it was a life: in the void. For the rest it was non-existence. Wragby was there, the servants . . . but spectral, not really existing. Connie went for walks in the park, and in the woods that joined the park, and enjoyed the solitude and the mystery, kicking the brown leaves of autumn, and picking the primroses of spring. But it was all a dream; or rather it was like the simulacrum of reality. The oak-leaves were to her like oak-leaves seen ruffling in a mirror, she herself was a figure somebody had read about, picking primroses that were only shadows or memories, or words. No substance to her or anything . . . no touch, no contact!

POLLY One of the best things at school was sitting around at lunchtime on Mag's desk singing together, wasn't it? 'Who's sorry now . . . Whose heart is aching for breaking his vow?' I can remember all those songs, and the sound of a lot of the girls' voices. We copied people like Brenda Lee and Connie Francis, or the rasping, nasal sound. But we did not hanker after being musicians in a group like all boys seem to.

HEATHER We were never really into Elvis – he was not our style. Nor was Cliff Richard – too goody-goody. We were as much impressed by the latest film as the latest pop record. Polly's and my satchel were covered with names like Dirk, rather than Cliff or Elvis.

POLLY We grew up in times when adultery was still a naughty word, when there were stories of women being sacked for adultery with their bosses, and when living in sin sounded incredibly romantic and wicked. Girls were sent down from universities for having men in their rooms. We didn't want to be like the spinster schoolteachers, nor did we want to be what we still called bluestockings, or even worse, suffragettes. We assumed we'd go on to do something interesting career-wise, though no girl dared mention the word career because 'career-girl' was still the worst label ever to get thrown at you.

We fondly imagined we would find ultimate happiness as the wife of some bohemian male genius. We knew we wanted to belong to the creative world, but never assumed for a moment that our own creativity would get us there.

I said 'I'm never going to be the great painter or writer, but I know I want to be married to one to help him with his work.' Except, though, I could imagine being an actress. I always knew I could do that myself, perhaps because being an actress is the easy way. It's the passive role, the actress is the writer's and director's puppet.

GEORGINA A lot of our self-projections were of the same kind. It was a question of finding a man who most expressed the kind of life you would like to lead and leading it through him. Interesting that we never for a minute imagined we'd create our own lifestyle. That's why it's still hard to keep it up today. It was a pattern set up right back then, and the hardest to break.

POLLY My own development began with the Easter Ban-the-Bomb marches. My sister and brother went on them and I associated Aldermaston with my sister's black stockings and straight skirts when she came back from London. I wasn't political, though, at all.

GEORGINA I was aware of Cuba in the autumn of 1960. The Cold War had really hotted up and I noticed *that*. Suddenly, after the Easter when Yuri Gagarin launched our minds into space as the first man in space, and a handsome one at that, we were back at school when the biggest scare we knew – or have known since –

blew up: Cuba. I remember the day. We didn't believe we would be alive beyond that afternoon. It's surprising how fear heightens the senses. It was warm and springlike; the sap must have been rising. We had a new obsession at school now, ogling male visitors. Mag had fixed her eye on a window cleaner and was determined to make him notice. We told her that she was stupid as we'd all be dead in an hour or two, having wrongly worked out what the time distance of the 2 a.m. deadline would mean in Burton-on-Trent.

POLLY Christ, I hadn't a clue about Cuba that day. So much for my political awareness.

GEORGINA In the morning, we decided on our plan of action. We had discovered there was a secret tunnel in the school, a sort of hidey-hole. Nothing glamorous like a priest's hole – the building was not old enough – but a hole at least. When we heard the bomb warning, the plan was that two or three of us were to rush down to the sweet shop and stock up on Toffee Crisps, Fudges, Rolos and chocolate bars, enough for our survival, and we'd hide in the hidey-hole! We had been brought up not only reading 'Wendy and Jinx' in *Girl*, but playing in old air-raid shelters left in neighbours' gardens; with the air-raid siren testing once a year; with fear at TV news; with talk of the Cold War and Civil Defence drill about how to take your Baked Beans down into your special shelter, which no-one had. The film *On the Beach* had been considered too frightening, too obscene, for most of us to see. We knew it could happen. We knew it was all a possibility.

At lunchtime, we decided it was ridiculous that we had to have lessons just before the end of the world. Especially as we had German just after lunch with a silly young girl straight from college, we usually had her in tears by the end of the class. We idled through German, sitting on each other's desks, chatting. Mag said she was going to grab the window cleaner in with us if The End came because she just had to know what sex was like before she went. We all secretly hoped she would pass him round. We sang 'Who's Sorry Now?' meaning we were sorry we'd been so prudish and had missed out on the Great Experience while the ones who'd had it looked smug. But the bell went for the end of German and then we had physics, and that teacher wouldn't let us play around.

As for politics as a whole? I remember reading about the race problem in America and that we'd sit discussing it. But we had very little exposure to the real problems in our cushioned lives. No black people around in those days, not even any Jews.

POLLY The only thing I was interested in was the rise of the new star, Terence Stamp, then a twenty-one-year-old Cockney boy, and the fact that *Billy Budd* was coming to Burton the next week! That summer, Nureyev jumped to freedom in Paris and he became my fantasy man for ages.

HEATHER But one late November afternoon, when we were fifteen, Mag and I used the fog as an excuse to get home and skip the hellish after-school ballroom dancing class with the local boys' grammar school because there was a new group going to be on TV for the first time. Somebody, the day before, had smuggled their new single into school. It was 'Love Me Do' They were the Beatles. And we were ready to break out – with their help.

3 Breaking out

There is an entry in my diary for early 1963 which says 'Pattie's catalogue for guitars has come.' It's something of a joke looking back, but if there was one thing the Beatles did for us, it was give strength to our dreams of getting out of the straitjacket, into the wider, more interesting world. The lazy singing of pop songs became more earnest as we actually wrote down the words of the Beatles' songs and practised them round at Pattie's house. (She only really became Pattie rather than Trish after Patti Boyd of course.) Heather, Polly, Georgina, Mag, Pattie and myself lined up in their sitting room while her mother was out at work, determined to be a female version of the Beatles. We even had a name: The Ravens. This imagined group gave us each a sense of identity. The taller, shyer ones were at the back on the imaginary drums, or playing the ghostly guitars (we hadn't a musical clue between us) and the more daring ones took up their positions at the front. Mag, naturally, was the flamboyant singer who crooned into the microphone and moved her body round, getting all the narcissistic kicks from her imagined audience. In our fantasies, we wanted to meet the Beatles one day, have a sporting chance of getting off with them. It seemed reasonable that the only people who really met the Beatles were other singers. The Ravens didn't get very far as not a single one of us could even sing. But it fed our fantasies through mock 'O' Level. 'I want To Hold Your Hand', 'Please Please Me', 'She Loves You' . . . they were our songs. The Beatles were ours too.

No pop star had ever taken on in the same way the Beatles did. In a way, it was as if the Beatles were directly for us. They appealed to the intelligent girl as well as to the 'others'. They were witty and bright. They were irreverent and independent, and they had emerged from their working-class homes to conquer the world.

We forget that the Beatle haircut was actually long-haired and bold then. They did create a whole new style, and I can remember feeling very marked out being the only girl in town with a Beatle jacket. It was in black suede and bought with my first Saturday-morning job earnings, along with my first pair of black, knee-length 'kinky' boots. The Beatles gave us a model for decadence, the Cavern in Liverpool.

In Burton, when we should have been studying for 'O' Levels in 1963, we began to go down the Kavern club there. On the door it said the Kavern Koffee Bar. It was under the Silver Spoon Café, near the bus station. It was underground and as nasty as could be. It was the nearest we could get to the real thing in Burton. Dark, hidden and dismal. It was also important that we should not have been going there.

On Friday evenings, I supposedly went to a Drama Club, where we were play-acting amateur Shakespeare, nurtured by our love for actors in Stratford-on-Avon. But one of the group went down the Kavern and reported back. My mother knew, though. All she could do was ask me to be careful and, no doubt, hoped I'd do nothing to ruin my reputation. Yet she didn't stop me going out. That kind of parental authority had already vanished. You went out and suffered the rows. Or you went out and they quietly prayed you'd be all right.

After the Kavern, the fairgrounds, and the dance halls, the next lure was the beatniks. We began going to folk clubs to hear their ideas. Dylan happened at that time and I know I got carried away just to hear the sound of his voice; the rasp, the wail, and the comments about war and peace, going to New York, Greenwich Village, coffee bars, people helping each other. That was the world I wanted.

I was interested too in Kerouac and Ginsberg, though, like many a great mind of my generation, I never finished one of the books, just read a few pages to say I'd done so. Dylan marked the beginning of our real self-identification – as a generation – not as girls. It was through him we broke away from our parents, and what we saw as their mistaken values. Donovan sang 'Catch the Wind' and we tried to do that too.

In 1963, the Profumo affair blew up and, as I was then living in Stratford-on-Avon, it was rather like living in Peyton Place with the lid blown off. It felt as if we were all Christine Keelers caught red-handed. Christine herself was fascinating, though we felt she had let our side down. She exposed the other side of the new free sexuality – even if hers was paid for – and the hypocrisy involved. No-one took Christine, her hopes and fears for life, seriously. She was the game, the pawn.

David Frost was the hero of *TW3* at the time: Stephen Ward was our hero, as the decadent man, badly wronged. But the Great Train Robbery caught most people's imaginations. Hemlines were going up and up and up. Kennedy was assassinated in the autumn and Swinging London was happening – in London.

We were moving into the era of the English-girl look – with Patti Boyd, Julie Christie and Tania Mallett. We began to ladle the make-up on: thick pan-stick and black lines round our eyes, like Dusty Springfield's. But it all began with the Beatles.

HEATHER I know what it was. Because they were a group, for the first time it meant we could share them between us as a group of friends, with no rivalry.

GEORGINA We would sit around for hours discussing which one we loved most. It usually worked out pretty fairly as girls tend to go round in groups of three or four. I wavered in my affections between John and George. If you went for John, you were declaring an interest in his arty bohemianism, but also being brave because he was so independent, so careless of authority, so rakish – a dangerous man. George was the more ethereal arty type, with a beautiful hollow cheek-boned face, spiritual and poetic. Paul was soft and romantic and Ringo was the vulnerable little boy who needed love, support and help but who would be incredibly loyal once he was yours. Heather went for John; Polly for George; Pattie for John too. Mag didn't care, she'd have them all.

ME I saw them in Cheltenham, when they came to do a concert there. It was a night fraught with hysteria and tension. I was in such a hurry not to miss the coach taking us all to Cheltenham that I didn't care that the bike I borrowed had no lights. When I was stopped by the police I told them not to be so stupid. I got a caution and to my embarrassment the next day a visit from the local inspector. But wild horses would not have held me back that night. I was going to see the Beatles. It was going to be exciting. Of course we didn't go with boys. They would have held us back. Just a few of us girls went and the Beatles got us all screaming.

I don't remember much about the concert, just the noise. Everyone screamed and for a while I sat with the distinct feeling that I was the only person not screaming in the whole hall. It was rather like being on the Big Wheel. When that goes hurtling down, out of control, you have to scream to release yourself. Screaming, hysteria, knicker wetting, they're all related. All a beautiful release for bottled up sexual energy. What did women in the past do with it?

GEORGINA I went to see the Stones at a concert in Manchester when I was in my mid-twenties and found myself so excited, jumping up and down, screaming, grooving to Jagger's hips, that I very nearly wet myself then, at 25! In fact, I always enjoyed seeing the Stones more. When I was seventeen, Ellie and I got tickets to the Mod Ball at Wembley where the Stones were playing, stuck out on a platform in the centre of the stadium. We had dancing tickets even, which meant we could get really close. I doubt if the Stones ever played so near their audience again. I can remember their terrified faces, when they were trying to get off the stage, surrounded by the heaving, maniacal, screaming mob, while the huge bouncers tried to hold us back. I even touched Mick Jagger's grey Marks and Spencer's jumper and my hand felt like gold dust. The only other memory of that concert was watching Manfred Mann. We were both shocked to see how much pan-stick make-up Paul Jones used to cover his acne. Just like we did. It made it look much worse. Just like ours too!

POLLY The words of the Beatles' songs worked for us too. We saw ourselves in the songs in the same way. At the time, there were lots of great rock n' roll songs around: like Del Shannon's 'Little Town Flirt', the Four Seasons' 'Big Girls Don't Cry', and Brenda Lee's 'All Alone Am I', but they were all American singers, and the words went with big cars, Cokes and hamburgers. The Beatles were all ours, from a Northern town, and we in our provincial towns all over the country could understand them. It's strange now to think they talked in the language of 'wack' and 'gear' and that we loved it. We loved them and devoured every word written by them. They were our fantasy men, fantasy lovers and fantasy friends. I often used to talk to John or George, alone in my bedroom, act out some scene, ask their advice on what they thought about my dress, hair, etc.

HEATHER When we should have been studying for our mock 'O' Levels, we began to go down 'the Cave', as we called it in Burton. Though actually on its door it was called the Kavern Koffee Bar.

GEORGINA It was the winter of the Big Freeze and my mother was all alone in our house as my father had to go away for his job. We had no heating, no running hot water, and we had to fish water out of a natural well in the garden when we could. Many a night we had to sit through power cuts as the power stations went out of action with the extreme cold. But, Polly I think it was, first went down the Kavern Koffee Bar and reported back. Soon, I was disappearing down the Cave. My parents knew, but said nothing.

The Cave was full of rockers, of course, and their women. Tough working-class Burton youths and girls with names like Sammy and Les, Jinxy, Beryl, Brenda, Maureen and Rosie. To me, they were like characters out of Mirabelle and Valentine. You could watch their passions. They weren't shy. Fights broke out as easily between the girls as between the men. I won't forget the day one dark-haired girl stood up, eyes flashing as she fixed her gaze on another girl's engagement ring and spat out, 'I've got something of his you haven't,' looking down at her stomach. Those girls challenged us to a fight once on the steps leading down to the Cave. I remember watching them screaming and tugging at each other's hair as they laid into each other – the first and last time I've really seen women fight. The boys came in and saved us. Polly reckons I saved us from being dragged in but I don't remember that. It was really exciting going somewhere so forbidden, so nasty.

The guys down the Cave were exciting too, of course. Earthy, dramatic, and very sexy looking with wild dark eyes, black greasy hair brushed back, and wild temperaments. We did not actually want to get too close to them – they were terrifying – but we did want to brush nearby. There was a group of rockers who went down the Cave – Bill, Sam and their crowd, who we did get to know because they also played in a band. They were tough working-class lads, but because they were musicians they were also sensitive, and to us fascinating. And they were all very good looking too. Because they were wild, they were exciting. But we never knew how far we could go with them without getting more than we'd bargained for. So it was always two steps forward, two steps back. They were the first boys, however, who made us feel like real girls. We wanted to dabble in the whole sea of sex and emotions, although we were by no means ready to wade in and get our feet wet then.

HEATHER We got involved with Bill's crowd, if you remember, because they were different, because they were protective towards us. But also, and this is important, they gave us the opportunity to go round with each other. I mean the reason I didn't want to go steady in those days was because I *did* have a better time with my girlfriends and you realize that going steady you get cut off the group. Bill's friends introduced us to all sorts of things – like the bowling alley! I ended up with Sam. He had a motorbike and I was quite turned on by it. I remember wearing black patent shoes and a very tight skirt, perched on the back of it. Going down the bowling alley had widened our social circle and I started going with a real rocker then. He was amazing. He had long, black greasy hair, was head to toe in black leather and wore a scarf across his face. I used to perch on the back of his bike, with no crash helmet or anything, and we used to do the ton. I think it was because of Mag that I got involved in this whole racy working-class thing. But also because I knew it was only a game and I'd never end up with one of this crowd. It was purely for excitement. Another of the guys I went out with had me round the back of the bowling alley and said he wanted to marry me. I nearly killed myself laughing. He was a farm labourer and I said 'Why me?' and he said because I was the best. That's another thing, we felt so self-confident with those guys because we knew we combined female attractiveness with the fascination of brains.

POLLY The Kavern was the place we slipped out to from school, in the lunchtime, to go and twist for half an hour. That was all part of it – being deliberately rebellious, breaking the rules laid down either by school or home. 'Nice girls don't go down such places.' We had to go. The Kavern was the place I stayed at too late, so I had rows with my dad back home about where I'd been. I wasn't that bad, but I had to do very little to get him into a state of anxiety. I began to change then, desperately wanting to become a rebel, a beatnik, myself, so I wouldn't have this grammar-school middle-class girl image any more. I wore a lot of make-up, grew my hair long, wore jeans with bells on the ends and floppy sweaters – the whole beatnik trip.

'Cave music,' I wrote in my diary that year: 'There Goes my Heart Again', 'I Like It', 'Lonely Boy, Lonely Guitar', 'Rockin' Crickets', 'Falling', 'Wamboo'. It is amazing to look back and realize how innocent it really was. Only a coffee bar, no purple hearts even, in those days. And how fantastically evil I thought it was.

GEORGINA The boys who worked the fairgrounds had the same kind of appeal. Burton had the Statutes Fair once a year. And Stratford had the Mop, when you moved there, Carol. Fairs were like a magnet. The rock music belting out, the Whip and the Big Dipper, the Big Wheel and the Wall of Death spelled out a sort of sexual excitement, laced with a hint of violence in the air, of mystery, of adventure. The most exciting place was usually on the Whip, which was really unbearable, but some greasy-haired, inevitably handsome, evil-looking young guy would always give a group of girls a thrill by striding over the insecure, moving floorboards and mastering the movement of the chairs. Coming up to us with a slow look through his half-closed eyes, with an effortless flick of the wrist, he'd give that chair an extra spin, saying of course, in his silent way, that he could spin us off into just that kind of excitement himself if we were game enough to give in to him. There we were in our stretch slacks, with head-scarves tied behind our necks, or in dresses with full petticoats. We weren't really ready to give in.

Why was it always these evil, dangerous men who lured us? We used to ask each other even then about it, already worried that we'd gone too far. What was wrong with grammar-school boys? There's an entry in my diary of 1964 about my new friend Ellie and me: 'Ellie wants to go to some dances with those grammar-school boys we met, and they want to go with us. I can't believe her! They were all right to talk to, but not to go to dances with! They're all serious and clever and deadly earnest.' Just then, those boys had nothing to offer me other than a repetition of my own dull life at home.

POLLY I remember the Statutes Fair. It was the one *big* occasion of the year. All the nastiness, danger, excitement had come to town. Fairground people are wanderers, and because of that they excite and threaten small-town people. Our parents had to let us go. There was nothing they could do to stop us. We didn't get up to much anyway. But to us it was heaven. Most of my thrills came from fantasy, I suppose. I'd go with Heather usually, Mag sometimes. But she was a bit frightening really.

We'd get there about nine I suppose; it would be all dark, and the lights would be ablaze, the cheap tinny music blaring out, enticing us in. All we tended to do was mill around. It's being on the hunt for the boys, staring at groups of boys, saying. 'Which one do you fancy?' that gives you the thrill. I was at a fair the other night and got a whole sense of nostalgia watching the gangs of girls hanging around, knowing just what they were feeling.

A group of us would wander between the Waltzers, the Whip, the Dodgems. I'd be keeping an eye open for the guy I fancied at the time. But this was fresh fantasy. We kept away from the Big Wheel or the Wall of Death. The Waltzers or the Whip were our best bet. I'd whisper to Heather 'Get him!' and there'd be some *beautiful* man, tall, lean, lank dark hair, just greased back but falling over his deep, sad eyes, a confident walk, thin shoulders, thin hips, careless mouth. Heather would go 'Uh, huh' which meant he'd got to her too, in the guts. We'd just stare, feeling very 'little me-ish'. But we were made for the evening. It's easy to pass hours just ogling a guy like that. You don't really want *him*, but you do want the fantasy. I'd be dreaming away of how the bloke on the Whip'd give me a turn and touch my hand. Our eyes would meet with a blaze. He'd raise one eyebrow slightly, which would mean, 'see you later'. Or he'd slip a piece of torn up ticket in my hand, that was clutching the side of the rickety seat, on which he'd have scrawled (though he probably couldn't write!) 'Come to the ticket booth.' And I'd hurry the ride round, and whisper to Heather I had to go to the Ladies, and walk in a dream over to him. He'd look down into my eyes with those brooding eyes of his and say 'I've never seen anyone so pretty.' And I'd fall into his arms. From then on, of course, I'd go and live with him. Say goodbye to my middle-class life, sod 'A' Levels and the sensible life, and I'd be part of the fairground world.

Neither Heather or I ever got near the men – we were far too shy looking. Mag got off with one. We were absolutely amazed. He sold tickets on the Bearded Lady. (*laughter*) He put his arm round her and said 'You're little n' cuddly,' and she said 'Ooh, get off.' But he started to kiss her and she let him, more so she could tell us what it was like. She came back from the woods with a huge love bite and the status of being able to say he wasn't up to much. 'He was boring, just a mechanic doing it for a holiday job,' she told us all in a little group afterwards. 'What's on your skirt then?' I remember asking her, staring at this dried, white, cakey stuff on the front of her skirt. Mag glanced down and blushed: 'Oh, shut up,' she said. We all knew what it was. She was too embarrassed to talk about it. We were very critical of each other really. That wasn't something you let happen. That was sordid. We were after a little romantic adventure, not the nasty bits.

Another rather too real adventure happened one night after a fair when there was a group of about seven of us, nice little grammar-school girls, and we were followed out of the fair by a gang of rocker girls in leather jackets, with bicycle chains in their handbags. They challenged us on the edge of the fields. One said to Heather,' 'Ere, you called something after my mate on her bike.' Heather said 'No, I didn't.' The rocker girl came back with 'Are you calling my mate a liar?' The only way out of it was to make out Heather was very vulnerable in some way. So we said she was nearly blind and must have mistaken her friend. As soon as we seemed weaker, not only did they drop the challenge but they turned quite sympathetic. When they said 'Have you seen Gloria?' though, we were quick to say 'Yes, that way!' I knew a girl who was beaten up by them, for looking a minute too long. They were rough, those women.

GEORGINA It was all the same at the dances too, wasn't it? We progressed from dances at church youth clubs, to the local village-hall hops and then to more commercial rock n' roll dances in dance halls like Hippodromes and Meccas. We'd go in groups of three or four, dance together, jiving sometimes, but more happily twisting, or doing the Shake. Ellie and I enjoyed dancing together. Sometimes boys would push in and dance with us – usually rockers or greasers. They operated in couples too, hanging round the edge of the dance floor, picking out a couple of girls and eventually forcing their way in between us, splitting us up and trying to take over. We didn't always want boys to move in, though sometimes it was a relief to be *seen* dancing with a boy, if it got rid of the tag of being odd for always dancing with your girlfriend. Ellie and I loved it all.

We'd spend all week working out what we'd wear, comparing notes about clothes. I remember it was before the days when jeans had come in. One dance, in particular, I can see myself. I had a navy blue M&S pleated terylene skirt, a pink, thin wool round-necked jumper – you know, the M&S style – and a navy blue Orlon cardigan. I thought I was It. Ellie was more arty looking, because she was doing art 'A' Level. It rubs off. She was wearing a John Lennon cap, that's it. Anyway, Saturday night was our big night together. When other tamer girls were going out with their boyfriends, we went off to those dances. We paid our way in, never bought a drink or anything, and went straight out there into the centre, like a bull ring, to dance. It was all the Everleys and the Beatles. We'd jive a lot together. That kept the boys away, as no-one jives with strangers. And we'd twist. You'd get boys coming to dance with you then. I remember when 'Can't Buy Me Love' came out. We did our own jump jive. We used to jump ourselves silly. I remember, too, winning a competition for the Shake once. I won a pound. We had so much energy.

We must have been odd, though. For one thing, we were out of our own class. These were all working-class boys and girls, and we were like interlopers. What were two 'A' Level girls doing among them? It's sex really. They gave us a sexual thrill, even though we never went near them. Once we were approached, or half way picked up, we had a problem. You know what happens at those dances. The guy just moves over and in, chewing gum, and letting drop the words 'wanna dance?' through a snarl. Oh, I love it still! It *was* exciting, that's all I can say. Anyway, that music was a sexual thrill in itself, driving and racy.

There was a great togetherness about it all. We worked out intricate eye language to tell each other what we felt. There was the quick glance that meant 'let's get the hell out of here'. Or the worried one when Ellie had pulled a good looking boy and wanted to stay with him. And then there were my moments of panic about what I would do. Did I stay with the ugly one? Make excuses and leave him? Then what? Without my friend I was on my own, wandering round the edge of the dance floor pretending I didn't care. Or, there were the times it was me who pulled the nice one, and turning traitor on her, chased after Ellie and begged her to stay with his mate so I didn't have to leave mine. Worse, was when I turned a blind eye on her misery, wished she'd go home, and turned on the smiles and chat to the new, fanciable one. At most, I suppose, Ellie and I would hold hands with one of them, or agree to be there at another dance, another week. Then we'd skip off home as fast as we could, in case they threatened anything like walking us home. We didn't want them to know where we lived. And we didn't want our fathers to see us walking down the road with some long-haired lout.

I was at one of those dances the night Kennedy was killed. It was in a village hall, though. There was a pathetic local rock group, playing sub-Merseysound, and some boring people hanging around. But it was our Friday night out. The news had come over earlier, but we'd waited all week through school for

46

this. We'd all gone out just the same. Everyone felt bored and irritable. Why should our Friday night dance be ruined because he'd been killed? No, we knew he was important. He was our hero too. The rock group didn't play long. We all sat round whispering and talking instead. No-one dared talk loud.

The most you could ever hope for at a dance was to be picked out by one of the visiting pop group.

HEATHER You're telling me. When I was fourteen and fifteen I used to go to dances with Mag, church-hall dances. I was never one of the pretty ones, and she tended to get off with someone while I tended to walk home alone. One dance, though, I can remember so clearly, down to what I was wearing – even the fact I had on very, very pearlized lipstick. My hair was awful as I'd just had it cut for my sister's wedding. I wore this brown shantung silky-look blouse with a ruffle, and a brown skirt, both from M&S. The skirt was turned over three times at the top – knee-length – and, over that, a white cardigan from my confirmation class. I had flat, white, square-toed shoes with a bar and stockings – I should imagine they were American Tan from Marks – everyone wore those, didn't they?

We all danced in a circle, doing the Twist. That had saved me because I couldn't jive, so I didn't feel such a fool. All of a sudden, I felt somebody pull my hand. This guy took hold of my wrist and I found myself dancing with him out of the circle. He had dark hair, brushed back, but it fell forward, like Cliff Richard I suppose. He was very self-confident and he was nineteen. He danced with me and then asked me if I'd go outside. He was the singer in the group and said he was from Derby. I was so impressed. I knew it was coming! That was the time I had my first kiss. I acquiesced quite confidently – as long as he didn't catch on I'd never done it before! He walked me home and I stood at the gate thinking 'Good heavens, this is what it's like to stand at the gate with your boyfriend.' I also thought 'I'm all right now. I've pulled someone and it's someone nice looking.' I was very cool and he said he'd ring me.

GEORGINA I had a pop singer experience too. It was pre-Beatles, when I was fifteen and suffering agonies at one of the boys' grammar-school dances. I felt very much that I wasn't one of the pretty ones; I was extremely shy and lacking in confidence. But my mother had made me a special dance dress. It was bright, midnight blue, in some shiny new material and really not a bad dress, considering. I wore white, high-heeled semi-stiletto shoes, and felt for once I didn't look pale and boring, but that the blue showed off my fair hair. I hated those dances with a vengeance. At those more formal occasions you could not gang up with your girlfriends and dance together but had to hang round the edge, waiting to be asked. I couldn't bear it because I did not fancy the boys, except one or two of the prefects who would never have come up to me, so I found a way out by hanging round the front of the stage pretending to be 'sent' by the music and the group. They were playing requests when I heard the singer's voice say it was for the 'girl in blue'. I looked round blushing, realizing I was the only girl in blue. Afterwards he came and talked to me. I was in heaven. I'd been picked out by the singer – it made up for everything. He was twenty-one and from Solihull. He bought me a drink and limply held my hand, then gave me a little card with his name printed on it. I shoved it in the bottom of a drawer when I got home knowing I never wanted to see him again. Still, it was an electrifying moment.

ME Rockers, or greasers, at dances, and fairground boys might have been all right for the thrills. But the kind of boys we really wanted to *get off with* were rather different, weren't they? We wanted the beatnik type. The coffee bar in Stratford-on-Avon, where I had gone to live at sixteen, called the Pit, was already in at the beginning of the 'beat' circuit. St Ives, Brighton, or Folkestone, and Stratford, were the places where the beat with his roll and newfound philosophy temporarily landed. There is an entry in my diary that reads, 'Finished up in the Pit, where we had to listen to J. D. a so-called beatnik, talking about Chelsea, drugs and contraceptives. Rather annoying, as we were supposed to be impressed by it all! We were!' But then J. D., I remember, was far too near home to have anything interesting to say.

POLLY I remember *the* party in Burton where I first spotted a guy wearing not only a green parka, but also a CND badge. He talked to me and it was the first exciting party I'd ever been to. There and then, in 1963, I promised myself I'd escape to London as soon as possible, to be nearer those interesting men who belonged to CND and who lived dangerously.

I was obsessively in love with Kev, the only beat in town who spoke to me once, only once so far. That Easter, I heard he was on the Aldermaston march. In my misery I wrote: 'He's on the CND march – a good thing I suppose, he's putting on weight. Broke up today. Please, please me, Kev, and be in town to-morrow afternoon in the Wimpy Bar when I am . . . oh how I wish I was there – camping out on the first step from Alder-maston. I wonder where he is now? I'd be keen to do anything if he was with me . . . saw some gorjus CNDers on tele. Wish v.v. much I was on the march – feeling utterly bored.' So much for political commitment in a seventeen-year-old dreamer!

GEORGINA The first thing we all did was arrange holidays in those other towns on the beat circuit – in Folkestone and St Ives. The winter of 1963, I first heard Bob Dylan. That was the new wave. The beatnik guys were in it and we wanted to experience it through them. Incredibly, my hearing of Dylan had nothing to do with any boys around. It was Ellie, already a bit of a bo-hemian herself, who said she had a record at home I might like. She was a bit ashamed of it as the singer sounded great, but the look of him on the cover of the LP didn't go with his image. I remember her telling me he didn't look as if he'd even shaved yet. He had a young, smiling, shy face, with peach-fuzz skin. He was wearing a brown suedette jacket, and had a silly cap on his head. In the slightly musty, damp atmosphere of Ellie's parents' flat we played it over and over again. We often used to go to folk clubs of course but that was only a way of getting out for the evening. We'd never heard this kind of stuff before. It was the first kind of music we listened to for its words!

Dylan's 'I'm a man of constant sorrow, I've seen trouble all my days . . .' Beatnik men put on the 'constant sorrow' style, pretended to a depth of despair they could not really know, and it was a great turn-on. I used to think, when I was seventeen, that only *men* could really feel deep, philosophical sorrow. I've always given them credit for genuine despair – so I used to fancy the moody type. All that angst and pain. Somehow we fondly imagined there were boys out there who also loved Dylan and Ginsberg, who would quote those lines to us.

ME Bob Dylan was very important for girls of our age. It was from listening to those early Dylan albums that I remember first catching a glimpse of contemporary woman. On *Bringing It All Back Home* he sings: 'She's got everything she needs, she's an artist, she don't look back . . . She's nobody's child, the law can't touch her at all.' All of a sudden, from those few words, I conjured up a new image in my fantasy life. 'She wears an Egyptian ring, it sparkles before she speaks . . . Bow down to her on Sunday, salute her when her birthday comes.' To know that Dylan loved that kind of woman, it was startling. It wasn't the Beatles moaning about teenage love. This was mature. It was spoken with utmost respect for the woman, who was an artist, who said things he wanted to hear, who had an individual identity. It was terribly important. The other song that had a similar effect on me was 'My love she speaks like silence . . . She doesn't have to say she's faithful, she's true like ice, like fire.' I must admit the line 'speaks like silence' hit me most because I knew I talked too much and envied those girls who managed to put on their enigmatic front, the all-female look. I still suffer from that envy too. I never have been able to stop talking too much.

Then there's another side, with lines of Dylan's such as '. . . my love she laughs like the flowers, Valentines can't buy her.' Dylan really marked the beginning of unisex feelings. Here was a man who could admit he liked women, as women, that he respected them. He was announcing a new world in which male and female shared experience; a gentler world with less of the old sex war. It was also Dylan singing 'Don't Think Twice, It's All Right', that made me blush with embarrassment to think how badly I'd dealt with the boys I'd known so far.

I once loved a woman, a child I'm told
I gave her my heart, but she wanted my soul
I ain't saying you treated me unkind
You could have done better but I don't mind
You just kinda wasted my precious time
But don't think twice, it's all right.

It was from Dylan I began to pick up the new politics and philosophies too, in my small town. He brought the news of the new way of thinking, didn't he?

Some people talk of situations, read books, quote quotations . . .
Some speak of the future. My love she speaks softly, she knows there's no success like failure and failure's no success at all.

Dylan marked our real self-identification – as a generation – not just as girls. Dylan also marked our real break with our parents, and what we saw as their world, their mistaken values. It was from Dylan I picked up the ideal of not being bourgeois. I remember Georgina, Ellie and I agreeing that we'd reject notions like engagements, marriage, smart clothes, make-up, because of Dylan.

GEORGINA I still have fond memories of St Ives. We were seventeen. I was at school and Ellie was at art school. We fixed up for ourselves to go youth hostelling (we told our parents) in Cornwall – hitch-hiking to us. Youth hostelling was the nearest we could come to complete freedom as girls. It meant we could pack up a bag of a few clothes, go by train to the first town, then hitch rides between youth hostels, stopping for as long as we fancied in different places. We weren't scared hitch-hiking together. We trusted people and expected them to be nice to us. On this, our first hitch-hike, one little old man asked us why we didn't carry at least a pair of scissors? The idea of trying to thrust a pair of scissors into someone made us laugh. Best not to think about that kind of danger and just hope it never happened. We had no idea of what we would do if ever we really did get stuck. Anyway we never did.

The high spot of that holiday was St Ives. We walked in singing, installed ourselves at the nearest youth hostel, dumped our bags and knew this was our mecca. The road by the sea seemed to be full then (but empty by today's standards) of long-haired beatniks, weirdos, artists, barefoot, casual, free people. We were shy and content to watch. We sussed out the central coffee bar and sat in there. We spotted three boys who looked interesting – one was tall with dark curly hair, one was shorter and stockier with long blond hair, and one I can't remember. To our amazement, we bumped into them in the pub that night. They came and talked to us and I know I fell silent in excitement (my love she speaks like silence . . .)! That night we went back to the hostel, though they'd told us they were sleeping out, under the arches on the beach, and we could join them if we liked. They were working-class lads from north London, not really our image of the beatnik, but on the other hand they seemed trustable. That night we talked it over. We were really excited at the idea but scared. Anyway, no use getting too carried away, they might not talk to us the next day.

We were on the beach with bags, carefully including our tooth-brushes, the next morning when they casually joined us. Ellie, I remember, was wearing jeans, and looked good because she had the newly fashionable shape – angular, leggy and boyish. They'd brought a football along and told us to join in with them. I felt lumpy, not at all lithe and interesting. Ellie had her sketch-book with her; I knew she looked more interesting than me. They asked us if we were going to sleep out. We looked at each other and one of us said 'yes'. It was extremely important, a real breakthrough point for us. Sleeping rough would be one notch on our belts towards becoming 'beat' ourselves. We went into town and bought a blanket, and they let us borrow some of their things. Then we took all our stuff and put it with theirs on the damp-smelling sand, under the arches. There were several others sleeping there. Couples rolling in the sand. Older groups who looked perhaps too wild. We were glad we had these boys with us. That evening we drank scrumpy in the fishermen's pub again, and went back to the beach where they lit a small fire and we sat around chatting.

The tall one obviously fancied Ellie. I didn't mind because I fancied the blond one by then, who was the most poetic. He was the one who sat letting the sand run through his fingers, while we gazed at the stars trying to remember things to tell each other about stars. He said we'd never know how many grains of sand were just slipping through his hand at that minute. Ellie and I were in ecstasy. I loved being on holiday with her because, des-pite my fears, I trusted her and she would never do anything like get off with one of those boys, leaving me to my fate. We weren't there for the 'getting off with' bit. In the end, we slept in a little group, them as shy as us, away from the others under the arches. Without proper sleeping bags, we had an uncomfort-able night. But who cared about sleep? We slept by the rocks, watching the stars, were befriended by a stray dog, and woken up in the end by one of the boys who was worried that the tide was coming in and we'd have to move up the beach, which we did. The next morning, we washed ourselves with all the other 'beat' girls in the Ladies' toilet, collected our things, went back to the hostel and, without really knowing why, we packed up, caught a bus, and moved on to the next town.

Later, we asked each other why we'd left so soon. Were we frightened of those boys? Didn't we want anything to go any further? No. We had had our beautiful experience in St Ives and if we'd hung around we were in danger of having it spoiled by reality. We were very romantic girls and what we'd had was better than any romantic dream. We moved along for another few days, dancing on beaches, shouting at the sea in our freedom, then decided to go home early as my parents were away and we could stay in their house on our own. We went to Birmingham, hitching there, so we could spend what was left of our holiday money on clothes. I loved all those first time sensations. And with my parents away for those two days, I wrote in my diary just one word – 'independence!'

ME If our real lives were plagued with who got off with whom at the local dances, or on holiday, our fantasy lives were still full of pop stars, film stars and now, nearer to home, actors. Thanks to my parents, and to the thrill of Polly, Heather and Georgina, I now lived in Stratford where we were actor mad. I call us 'actor groupies' but the timing has to be remembered. 'Groupie' then meant we hung around actors, wanted to get to know them, but not actually to sleep with them at all. We were only after experience and adventure. We were part of the group of middle-class girls who hung round Stratford, waiting at the stage door, sitting in the Dirty Duck (the actors' pub) staring at groups of actors. Maybe big-time pop stars would rate a more committed kind of 'group' activity. I can still fantasize even today about giving up my life to run away with some laid-back blond-haired Californian rock star!

GEORGINA Still happens. I went to a play in Stratford recently with a friend, and we stood in the Duck at the bar – I couldn't help it. I found myself fixing my eyes on the most fanciable actor I recognized, and despite the fact I know he's gay, I turned my incredibly unsubtle gaze on him, burning holes in the cheeks I so desired and, to complete the fantasy, felt sure he had noticed me! The actors were much more exciting than any home-grown boy. They came from London for the season. They were wordly-wise, experienced, decadent (the sexual ambivalence was fascinating and not too threatening), beautiful and glamorous. They had rich, booming voices, masses of self-confidence, talked about plays and acting and their careers, and were absolutely intriguing – *if* we could get near them.

POLLY They lived in various cottages around Stratford villages. We'd get invited back to parties, or for talk after coffee. We got our thrills from the atmosphere as much as anything real. All we did was sit in the Duck for long enough, a small group of us talking animatedly about the theatre, looking happy and laughing, and soon enough one, or two, actors who knew what we were there for, would come over and join us.

Then, when the pub closed, we would walk in a group over the bridge and along to the place, or get a lift in a car to some village. We tended to get split up at that point. Sometimes, I'd go off with one of them. Sometimes Ellie or Sue, who were less adventurous, not quite such risk-takers as me, would grab hold of my arm and say 'Where the hell are you going?' and I'd say 'It's OK,' hoping like hell it was. I didn't intend to lose that much . . .

ME I lived at home so it was different. I used to walk back in the dark, unlit streets, terrified, wondering why I never had any blokes who drove me round in their cars? The answer was obvious. We were out for our own ends. We were saying we were equals. And that meant walking home alone in the dark. It's only when you play the submissive role you get taken home in the end!

GEORGINA It was the summer of the Shakespeare Quatercentenary and the theatre was running the history plays, with *Richard II, Henry IV Parts One and Two, Henry V, Edward IV* (reworked by John Barton), *Henry VI* and *Richard III*. It was the first summer of David Warner, too, who, to his own surprise, and horror, became a pop hero for young girls – not least for Polly. We saw all those plays at least two or three times. It's much more fun going to see a play when you can sit and spot the guys you know or you fancy, or who you pulled the night before. You feel a cut above the boring audience.

POLLY I do it even now. I go to the theatre a lot and I'm always mad for someone in the play. I can't get rid of the habit. A play is really dull for me if there's no-one I can drool over in it. Of course, at seventeen, it meant I wanted to go into the theatre. I really thought I did. It took me years to realize my talent would be better used elsewhere. It's a good way for a girl to get to know interesting people though. It works too!

ME Virginity was our big problem. We still had it more or less intact. We wanted to keep it and wanted to lose it at the same time. We knew about sex, sort of knew what going all the way meant. But there was a lot of mystique about virginity and we had grown up with all the talk about not losing it. We all read magazines like *Honey* and took to heart, to some degree, articles about virginity and what to do. Even in 1963 they were running features like 'Why bother to say no?' If boys say 'If you really loved me you'd want to . . .' or 'It's old-fashioned to wait. We're going to be married eventually, aren't we?' *Honey* still says 'A girl is more likely to lose a boy than keep him if she lets him have his way: she begins by losing her own self-respect and ends up by losing him too.' And finally, 'It is one of the deepest instincts to want purity in a bride.' We didn't exactly see our virginity in those terms. The instinctive reaction to boys who 'wanted purity in a bride' was to say 'bugger them'. We had already gone beyond the idea that we'd be trading it in for marriage. But the question of who with and why, was nevertheless serious and was the point of endless discussions. Pregnancy was not even a part of it. We were way behind such sophisticated concepts. Actually losing your virginity was a difficult enough thought to begin with! We hadn't had much in the way of sex education, either.

GEORGINA At school, the summer we were fifteen, they put it upon the embarrassed, unmarried, woman biology teacher to tell us all about it. I remember she blushed, asked us what word we used for 'spooning' these days, and Mag, of course, shouted out 'necking'. The teacher blushed even more and proceeded to tell us about sex – what she called 'reproduction' – based on pictures of the frog and the dog. I drew those diagrams, copied down the notes, but was still mystified. I do remember, though, she told us not to play with ourselves 'down there' because we would dull the senses and would not be able to enjoy it with our husbands. I took her word on that. So any masturbation I got into as a teenager was tentatively through the material of a nightie! It made me hung up about touching myself there, of course. You know I honestly didn't know what the word 'balls' meant till I was eighteen and got a girlfriend to explain to me. And I carried with me the explanation about dogs through to the first boy who taught me about male anatomy. Until then, I believed that the male penis, rather like a dog's, would emerge red and rather horrid from a sheath.

ME We sounded a lot more experienced than we really were in those days. We were not in any way interested in holding on to our virginity as trading power and knew that our first lover was not likely to be our last. In fact, 1963 had a good object lesson for us in just that. England was just beginning to 'swing' – well, London was at least – when the Profumo affair blew up and shocked our small town, because of course Jack Profumo was Stratford's MP. It was almost as if someone had written Peyton Place about Stratford and was pointing the accusing finger at all of us. Christine Keeler exposed the new free sexuality – even if hers was paid for – and the hypocrisy involved. Stephen Ward said anybody who sold their body for money was, in fact, a prostitute, and that applied to women who married for money. We dug Stephen Ward – decadent, despairing, drugged! He fitted. But Christine Keeler had let our side down. The incident had some effect on how we worked out about when a girl should play her trump card of sex. Should we play for cash, goodies, gifts, marriage, security, drinks in the pub, and a lift home? Or was it better to offer it freely, expecting nothing in return? We're still finding out!

At the time, skirts were knee-length or on their way up. We were moving fast into the era of the English-girl look which Georgina took up most, perhaps because she had blonde hair. Jean Shrimpton had already become *the* model. It was also the time of Patti Boyd (just after meeting George Harrison on the set of *A Hard Day's Night*), and Julie Christie, and of models like Jill Kennington, Celia Hammond, Tania Mallett, and Grace Coddington.

GEORGINA I worshipped them all. Those were *my* days. Hair was blonde, worn straight, with a fringe, ironed if necessary. Looks were clean and uncluttered. Fresh faced and natural if Natural Wonder make-up can be called natural!

POLLY I wore pan-stick make-up and cover-up beige creams to cover my open-pored skin. Masses of eye make-up, thick black lines under and above the eyes, mascara, and pale whitish lipstick. Sometimes I wore deathly white make-up to be dramatic.

GEORGINA I remember only that I never learned to put make-up on properly. I would smear the tan coloured cream over my face all right, but then run out by the neck, so that the line wobbled round the bottom of my neck. I never did like make-up. I was sloppy and not very artistic and I could not put it on well. I also had very sensitive eyes, so the eyeliner and mascara would make them itch. I would rub them and end up with black smudges for eyes – the Dusty Springfield look. After a few years I gave it up for ever. But in the mid-60s I still had that fear of not covering up my spots, and of being seen naked without eye make-up or of looking pale and ill without the regulation black lines.

POLLY For me, the worst moment about spending a night with a guy, in the early days, was waking up in the morning and knowing he'd see me without my eye make-up on. I knew he'd go off me then!

ME It was all Cathy McGowan in those days too. She became the 'girl with her finger on the teenage pulse', on *Ready Steady Go*. She was hardly regulation pretty, though she did have that nice swingy hair.

HEATHER I used to iron my hair straight to get it like hers. I suppose I identified with her as I had dark brown hair and could make it look like that.

POLLY Rita Tushingham in *A Girl With Green Eyes* made the first grade of plain girls being seen as pretty because they were interesting, and gave us all hope. Julie Christie was, of course, very pretty but still she had a sulky mouth and wore no make-up in *Billy Liar*, and in *Darling* she put over the beautiful, carefree girl, lacking any sense of responsibility. I liked Françoise Hardy particularly because she wore no make-up, dressed very downbeat and sang about despair.

GEORGINA I used to read endless issues of *Honey*. I can remember individual issues of 1964 and 1965 because each page was devoured so carefully. It wasn't till I got to university and some guy laughed at me for reading rubbish that I shamefully stopped. I absorbed the fashions, the style, the look, out of envy really. There was one particular issue, April 1965, which I think set my own style for the next few years. It had a picture of Julie Christie on the front, looking very soft, with her lovely straight blonde hair, and her whole tone was a sort of violet, dusty blue. She was wearing a flower-printed, cotton shift dress, the kind we all had with a keyhole neckline. It was a static cover-girl picture, but it gave an image: short, above-the-knee dresses, pale skin, pale sling-back shoes, swinging blonde hair blowing out behind. It was the dolly look – and I tried it. By then Cathy McGowan was saying her skirts were five inches above the knee and mine slowly followed.

It happened quite suddenly, by that summer or autumn of 1965, the skirts shot up very, very high. And the funny part was, only the day before we had been wearing girdles and strict bras, not letting our bodies show. I remember very clearly the day I suddenly realized it was all right to show my body off. I had grown up with an obsession about my bottom, that it was too big and ugly, and should be disguised at all costs. I used to wear home-made shift dresses that were deliberately widened over the hips so as to hide the fact I had a bottom. I was brought up to restrict myself in girdles, so I often got stomach aches from them. I used to wear jumpers over slacks that fell outside the waistband just over the spring of the bum, so that it made it look as if I had one neat straight line, rather than any curve.

I came home one day wearing Ellie's too-small, very tight pair of corduroy jeans which wound their way round my curves, and with them a tiny jumper. I knew my bottom stuck out a mile – but I already knew that men fancied it and I wanted to be proud of it. My mother was cross, but then how was she to know I could cope with the dangers such provocation led to? I don't think I have anyway. But any girl who raised her skirts inch by inch to the point of no return knows what I mean when I say there was nothing more liberating than the feel of the wind, the air, rushing up between your legs, fanning your fanny. It was a childlike, innocent sense of freedom, I reckon. A freedom from restraint I felt as I skipped along in my dolly, baby-doll clothes, knowing that men could look up my skirt when I climbed to the top deck of the bus, or bent over to pick something up. Knowing that men's eyes were fixed on my legs and the glimpse, no longer of ankle, but of inside thigh and pubic hair, under my skirt. I hated to be told I was provoking men, even to rape, that I was teasing them. I'd assumed my own sense of freedom and some-how, I suppose, I expected them to understand it too. I wanted to be wide-eyed like Jean Shrimpton, pert-mouthed like Julie Christie, and I was not really expecting the criticism we all got for hoisting our skirts up.

ME '1965,' the paper said. 'It's a great year to be a girl.'

4 All you need is love

And so to sex. It's been there lurking behind all those other stories of hanging round coffee bars and fairgrounds, turning into actor groupies, hoisting our skirts up to crutch level. It was all to do with sex really. How we learned, experimented, ex-plored. What we felt. The fight to hang on to our virginity while desperately wanting to lose it. The never-ending battle between the physical and the social sides of ourselves.

GEORGINA Pattie took me to a youth club and one of the older, taller boys there who was actually in the sixth form, while I was only fifteen, began to walk me home and we started kissing. I don't remember much except I didn't particularly like him. I didn't like kissing him much either, it seemed very wet and rather distasteful and my mouth would be all chewed to pieces. He put his tongue in my mouth and I remember I wouldn't do it back to him. I don't know why. But I was rather ashamed of him, perhaps because he wasn't good looking, though I didn't rate myself either. There was no guilt involved, just vague dis-interest and relief I was on my way.

I used to let him put his hands up my jumper and got an incredible turn-on from the sensation in my breasts, or just from his hands round my back or midriff. I stopped wearing vests then, pretending to my mother that I wasn't cold and none of the other girls wore them. But I never knew whether I should let him put his hands up my jumper, whether other girls did, or if I was being a bit too bold. So, after a while, getting my pleasures,

I'd say 'no' and move his hands away. Even then, I used to feel the beginnings of those soft, sensual, groaning feelings – the desire to melt a bit. I can distinctly remember though, this one very sad occasion of competition between Pattie and me. She was much sexier looking than I was, and she had a boyfriend at the youth club who was the catch of the place. Steve came all the way across town, he was twenty, had a car – one of those big rocker Fords. He had greased, slicked-back hair, worked so he had money, wore jeans, open-necked shirts, and V-necked jumpers. He looked like Cliff Richard, with a relaxed manner and wide open smile. He had a terribly spotty face but because he was confident it didn't matter. He was working-class, a mechanic or something. Anyway Pattie got him.

She used to sail off home in his car, while I walked back with this other bloke, wondering how I could get my pleasure without being too put off by his smell and taste. That was my first awareness, and it's been important ever since – of that initial chemical balance – of either loving someone for his smell or hating it. One evening, at the youth club, Pattie's bloke, Steve, drew me aside and said he wanted to go out with me! I knew it was a big moment for me. To finish with the first bloke and get one up on Pattie. Oh dear! It all sounds so corny now, but at the end of the evening it was me sailing off in his car and she walking alone up the road. You have to go through these stages – but we made it up afterwards.

Anyway, Steve was something better. Again it was kissing and feeling my tits, but he was the first one who groaned a bit himself, and used to put his hand up my skirt. It was summer and I remember lying across the front seat of his car – you know, a bench seat (I laughed later when I heard boys call them 'grunt hunters') and that delicious feeling of him putting his hand slowly up under my blue cotton dress – up to there. I used to let him put his fingers up the side of my knickers and up inside me. I used to enjoy it. It would be quite wet even in those days. It was the same story, though. I had no idea whether I should let him or not. I was annoyed he often had dirty fingernails. I think I was aware he got more out of me than he had from Pattie – even though she looked the sexy one. But it also worried me in case I was too cheap – perhaps to compensate for not being pretty? I've always felt a bit whorey actually, because I don't *really* care what they think. But I knew I liked the sex.

I used to get these terrible stomach aches with Steve. You know, their eyes mist over as they work their fingers on you, and you're melting, but neither of you knows anything about coming, or bringing a girl off, so I'd end up pushing his hand away and I'd go home with this cramp right across my stomach, across the middle. I don't remember much, not even how it finished. Maybe we had exams and I'd have stopped going out.

HEATHER I've told you about my first kiss, the singer from the group. He said he'd ring me and he did. The next time I met him he had a rolled up raincoat and he took me on to the Rec. I was only fifteen, you know. He took me to the far corner of the Rec and spread his mac out and we lay on it. That was the first time I felt somebody against me. You know the *feeling*. Not so much that specifically. It was all right when he was lying on top of me but he did this thing of rolling over and pulling me on top of him. I used to sit up then. It was all very innocent really – no kind of groping down there. I'm trying to think what I got out of it. I can't remember. I took Mag along the next day and showed her where we'd been lying because it was quite something, the idea of actually *lying* down with a man on top of you. I think I was frightened.

GEORGINA Remember those warning lines about being frightened off when a boy starts breathing heavily for that's when he can't stop? I used to read that in *Woman*, and imagine they'd start panting and go into some hysterical frenzy.

HEATHER I did have this distinct feeling that it was all a number. I never really got a great deal out of sex until I got to a point beyond all that.

POLLY Alongside all the desperate curiosity, desiring in a way, wanting to kiss and touch, there was a definite 'get off' feeling for me. I went to a party with some dreadful upper-class, hunting type; I was sixteen and he was nineteen. He had a car and got off with me. I didn't fancy him. He took me down Marston Lane. It was all right to kiss him, but when he got round to feeling my tits and sticking his finger up me I didn't want it. Like when I was four I felt 'This is something I have to go through, I have to do.'

GEORGINA What on earth did we go for in the male?

POLLY Freedom. Why do we still do it, though? That's more the question. I know now that it's the fantasy male. The kind I fix my eyes on. The wanderer, the freak, who is impossibly hard to make relationships with. Maybe there's a part of me wants them because of that. They're not going to be good solid husbands at all. They're not going to make demands on me and are not going to control me. But it also means some part of me is the wanderer, the rebel, the artist. In us, in all of us, the male figure exists. I think that male principle in me is the creative, the sexual energy in me, all that extrovert thing.

GEORGINA But did you want sex then?

POLLY I *did* everything expected of me as a teenager of that time, all the heavy-petting number. But it didn't mean anything to me. Looking back – they did it all to me. Only when I began to do it to them I noticed I had something to give out. In the early days, they always wanted to go further than I did anyway. Just before I went to Folkestone, with Bill and Sam of the Kavern, I remember sticking my hand in Sam's jeans (I have a vague memory he may have put my hand there, not me?). It was the first time I actually got hold of a prick and I remember thinking 'My God, that's nice, I like the feel of this!' (*laughter*)

GEORGINA Then I went and pulled Bill. The high spot of my life. You know, I think my self-confidence began then – my coming out. Bill had short brown hair, cut in a Beatles style, and a nice tanned face. He was a building labourer, a rocker, and a guitarist – very sensitive. I knew it wouldn't last long as I was going away for the summer. So really I was only in it for kicks. It was gorgeous, and I just remember him taking my hand across to his jeans, the zip was undone and there was this hardness underneath the layer of jersey-knit cotton of his pants. I was so shocked. Rather mortified and cross that he'd forced that on me. But fascinated at the same time. It's a strong memory. I'm sure I never thought about going all the way. I knew nothing about erections. You know the language like 'stick it up yer' – but you don't know what it looks like. I was scared, and after letting my hand take in the feeling for a minute or two, I drew it away. When we went away that summer, I said to one of you: 'I hope I meet a boy I like soon. The ones I've been with so far I've not really *liked*.'

Nothing much else happened that summer. But by the time I came back I was suddenly a lot more confident. I began to go round with Ellie more because we were in different sixth forms. I took a Saturday morning job in a shop. There was this new guy in town, a bit the beatnik, a bit the wild gypsy, the first local boy I'd ever seen who was fanciable. He smiled, joked, had laughing eyes, was bright in an original way, had Beatle hair and a cap, was small, nimble, and a very beautiful person. He came into the shop one Saturday, with Ellie and another friend. They were going to a coffee bar together. He chased me round the shop and asked me out that evening. I was over the moon. They were both a bit cross at my getting him.

He was my first 'emotional' experience. I wasn't with him just for sex. He was a groovy guy, who I wanted to go out with, and I actually 'went out' with him in the real sense. It wasn't just necking sessions. It was going round together and having fun. I was so proud to be with him. He was so funny, jumping around and being witty. He didn't have a car and I only remember once propping up my front door with him. He kept telling me funny stories and making me laugh, and we were kissing and being warm to each other. He wasn't any sexual threat. He was the effeminate type. I don't think it was avoiding sex, but he was the type I adore. It's funny – I had it pointed out to me recently that the type of man I have good sex with I tend to treat as a sex object; I don't give him the warm, forgiving, affectionate side of me at all.

It's true. There seems to have been my adored type, and the ones I get a sexual thrill from, who frighten me, unnerve me, make me unconfident, demanding, and whom I finally push off. Anyway, this guy hurt me in the end by pissing off. He needed a screw I think and I was too straight, too tame for him. I tend to say 'You'll get bored with me when you find out how straight I am.'

After him? Depression. No-one for ages. Shame, humiliation, and boredom. Then a boy from university who was like the fifteen-year-old lot – boring, but sexy. He took me in his car to pubs and I went necking with him. I enjoyed his mouth. His body was too small for me to feel comfortable with. But I remember being on the Rec in the dark, letting him put his fingers up me,

63

when the police car shone its headlights at us to make us go home. I loved that! But nothing really – except I thought 'God, will I have to marry this kind?' My parents met him and obviously thought so.

What was your pulling power, Heather? You did better than us, though you say now you weren't one of the pretty ones. But we were very jealous of you. I think now it's when a girl knows her own sexuality that the latent confidence comes out. You were short-sighted though, and didn't wear glasses to dances, did you? It made you look very passive and dependent, real eyes-down and demure. We used to say behind your back, 'Oh Heather'll take her clothes off for anyone.'

HEATHER Really? I know Tom got off with me that day because I couldn't see him properly. It gave me courage to stare at him. Mind you, he couldn't see me properly either. But then as far as my sexuality was concerned, it was to do with finding someone who awakened it. All my sexual experience was crammed into two years. At sixteen I met John but didn't like his spotty face.

GEORGINA What did you think about kissing a spotty face?

HEATHER I couldn't do it. I didn't. No, I could not kiss a spotty face. Mind you, in those days we never actually appreciated a face and kissed it. With John, he took me out once, held my hand (that's all it was in those days) and said would I go out again and I said 'no'. He said he wanted to go steady with me and I told him I had better things to do! He said 'No-one else wants to go out with you!' Then I looked at him. It was my first realization that nothing is often better than anything!

Lying in the park with Sam, I think it was: that was when I first had my hand brought to the male and felt the hardness. Do you realize we were all introduced to that by Bill or Sam! Jesus, they've got a lot to answer for! (*Howls of laughter*) I dragged my hand away, because I couldn't cope. I never thought about 'going all the way'. In that sense we sailed very close to the wind in our innocence. The first person I let go right up there was Robert. I sent him a Valentine card. He was my only middle-class one. He was at university, and that was his status symbol. I was sixteen and he was good looking. He was the first person I got emotionally involved with, the first to put me down and the first one to stick his hand up my skirt. I remember thinking 'God, what must he think?' because I hadn't got nice knickers on. That awful self-consciousness you have at that age about freckles and spots, and knowing he knew what sort of underwear you wore. They didn't reciprocate in the same way, so they sort of got one up on you, didn't they? I stopped him though because I was pissed off about a blonde girl. I thought 'He's not getting going with me until I get a bit more from him emotionally.' In a way, it was to do with how far to let him go, because I remember pushing his hand down and I thought 'This is what you're supposed to do, you're supposed to let him go so far and then push his hand away.'

When I was seventeen, Polly, Mag, Sue and I went on our first holiday to Folkestone. We got a caravan and when we arrived found that Folkestone was *the* place to go for beats. We asked where the coffee bar was and were told about the Acropolis, so we went in and there were all these people wearing bleached jeans because that was the thing. (You held your jeans up and splattered bleach on them. I did it when I got back to Burton and I was the first person in Burton to do so. Also the first to have bell bottoms with bells on them!) We met Powerful Pierre in Folkestone, or at least, I met him. I must have been the puller then. Powerful Pierre had short blond hair. He was a Mod. They all took drugs, but we were very stuffy because when it came to it we said 'no'. He had this stuff in a sort of mesh – he sniffed it – I still don't know what it was. I said 'no thank you', partly because I didn't want to be seen to do it wrong.

Powerful Pierre rammed me up against the caravan. I'm sure a lot of my sexuality was repressed. I used to feel people sort of devouring me. He was the person who de-virginized me. He stuck his hand up me, really far, you know, rammed it up me. I can remember him saying 'You 'ain't 'ad it much 'ave you?' Presumably because I was tight. I don't know what I felt; it was too much of an onslaught. Up to this point I don't think I'd learned how to respond to men. I can remember sitting in the Acropolis watching a girl necking with this guy, passing her hands all over his back and everything. And I was thinking it looked a bit sort of false. Too much like doing a number. In that sense I don't think I was really into it, though I enjoyed it obviously. The next morning I went into the Ladies and of course I'd bled. I thought

'Great, now I can use Tampax!' because all those Tampax ads used to say 'even if you're not married'. No-one ever tried because one girl at school did and said it was like sitting on the Rock of Gibraltar. She couldn't get it in far enough. I got it in, but not as far as you do now.

Then we met some guys about to go off to university. Polly got the good looking one. Mag and I got the others. So, for the first time in her life, Mag learned to make a cup of coffee – to get away from this guy – and I fell asleep. Polly had her one coming all over her. She talked to me about it and said 'He wanted me to let him – should I?' I said 'No, because if you get pregnant it will reflect on all of us.' I'm sure I said that because I thought she was more experienced than me and I didn't want her to get any further ahead.

POLLY On that holiday in Folkestone, I was desperately hung up on Tim. One night, in that caravan, Mag resolved that one of us would get it that holiday, so she got the bed down for us, like a real Madame, and she was really encouraging me and Tim by pulling the screens across. The rest of them were having half-hearted snogging sessions. That session with Tim went as far as him getting his trousers off, and me with my knickers off, and a lot of fingers up and I think he actually did ejaculate. He enjoyed the hands, and he came. I remember there was a lovely feeling of the wetness of the body. Isn't it remarkable how far you could go in those days without actually doing it? I was really proud the next day that I'd got as far as that, seen and felt the whole thing, even if I wasn't prepared to actually do it. I told the others in very coy terms. You know how you do this whole mystique number? The fear of pregnancy must have come into it because I said 'He couldn't have done it to me anyway as he hadn't any precautions' – I meant a sheath – and poor Sue was shocked by what I meant. That I'd actually got hold of it in my hand. It's easy to say now – but to touch it!

HEATHER It's funny how selfless boys were in those days. They never asked us to bring them off, did they?

POLLY After that I got very preoccupied and obsessed with sex and desperate to have it. Kev got all the projection – my beatnik with long black hair. What chance did I have of getting him though, I thought, if I didn't bring out some of that rebelliousness inside me. My dreams then were for the real men, the 'faded blue jeans and long blond – or black – hair'. You coined that phrase, Carol.

GEORGINA We wanted really beautiful men, didn't we.

POLLY I remember at sixteen going to Paris, and the only thing I was interested in were the decadent looking bohemian types round Montmartre. The rest of Paris I could have stuffed. I just wanted my fantasies. Then, there was St Ives – with Georgina, Ellie and you – where for the first time I was able to walk through the streets barefoot, with my old black hat on. I felt quite lucky because I got the pick of the bunch there. We spent a heavy night in that caravan too! I can't remember the guy's name. Just the heavy snogging and touching each other, very erotic. I remember he had a thin, bony chest and this very fine hair all down his front. The upper part of their bodies was the really beautiful part – the mouth, the cheekbones, and the fine hair on the chest – but not down there!

GEORGINA In that sense my idea of a beautiful man is a very feminine man, actually. Is yours?

POLLY Oh, yes. It means something too. Feminine men are sensitive – they have a strong understanding of women because their animus is in control. They're not a sexual threat, these beautiful men – I mean they're not going to rape you. They're not terrifying. So I think there was an appeal to them and an appeal to the frightening ones as well – the ones who might fuck you. I remember getting very excited with Rod, which was the first time I became aware, even just with two pairs of jeans meeting on the floor, that something in him could rub against something in me and I went 'Oh, yes!' It was my first idea that sex itself, not just the romantic arms round and kissing, could be exciting.

GEORGINA Beautiful men! The spring of my seventeenth year, there was a new youth club I began to go to, and a new emotional experience. A young teacher of twenty-two fancied me above all the other girls there. I was in heaven. I think I looked more mature than I was, because I seemed self-confident. I fell completely for him and slipped, immediately, into my self-destructive ways. So I put myself down and felt sure he didn't like me enough. But it was the first time anything so romantic had happened to me. I thought he was beautiful, though he was rather solid – a rugby player, not the sensitive type. But he was intelligent and had fat lips and a broad smile! Did he set my heart strings going! It's all in my diary – bliss, rapture over the graveyard cleaning (we were all out on a youth clubs good-works expedition, but I was only aware of him that day). He took me for a drive in his car. It was a beautiful June evening, and he picked me a flower, a blossom from a tree. I don't remember one jot of the sex between us! Only the emotions. I imagine nothing very much happened because he probably wasn't a virgin and he'd assume I was. I can't imagine he'd have gone in for groping, being the religious type. You can't let out the grunts and groans on a church-goer.

It finished quickly enough because his father was ill and I wasn't seeing enough of him and I wrote him a letter saying so. He wrote back saying that as I was taking it so seriously we'd probably better not see each other again. I remember crying and crying in despair, by the church walls, cursing God out loud for letting me down with one of his henchmen!

Then St Ives that summer with you, Polly, and Ellie. I was like you, Heather, going back to school that autumn, I felt really terrified that I didn't seem to want to go out with grammar-school boys. Everyone seemed to have boyfriends except our little circle. And we stuck out as failures. So it was back to the dances. Oh! I nearly forgot Drew. He was my next big step, very big.

HEATHER You're very hung up on the social thing, aren't you.

GEORGINA I know. I can see it now. But I can't help it. It was Stratford next, visiting Carol. We'd all been out for the evening. I got picked up by this groovy looking guy with short blond hair and a deep voice. Drew was an actor of course. He asked me round the next Sunday for tea. So I stayed in Stratford longer, in order to go back and see him.

He asked me if I was a virgin and if I wanted to lose it. I said I didn't and he said OK. Then he unzipped his jeans. We were on his bed. I'd never been so close to a man – and as he was twenty-seven he qualified as a man – and he played with himself in his pants. Then he took them off and drew my hand over to his enormous cock and I was just terrified. He put his hand over mine and began to move it up and down for me, and said 'Like that, baby, keep it up like that, baby.' He did nothing to me at all, but I just sat there moving my hand up and down absolutely in awe of the whole experience. It took ages, I remember. Knowing nothing about a man, I'd get bored and slack off. He'd groan and say 'Keep going.' Part of me hated him for his self-centredness and part of me loved him for the decadence, for the brutality of using me in this way, of being at the end of the bed, like a slave. He could have whipped me, I think, and I'd have loved it. Then, in the end, he came. Amazing when it's your first time. He was big and purple. I felt real despair when he got near the point and he'd relax and lose it. I'd think 'Oh God, hurry up, I've got a stiff arm.' He never made me suck him off or anything. Thank God. I was fascinated by learning how the penis changes and feeling it fill up. Feeling the movements as the semen came and shot over his stomach. I worshipped him and the experience.

POLLY You were being used!

HEATHER I went back to school at seventeen feeling 'Why is it I'm not attracted to grammar-school boys?' There must be some who are attractive! After the Folkestone holiday, I was a lot more sophisticated. Then I bumped into this guy wearing bleached jeans like mine. We stared at each other like soul mates. Now he was a fascinating guy, because he was a drug addict! He was from London, hiding out, cooling off. He was the first person who said to me: 'I'd love to have sex with you.' I found that a real turn-on, much more than anyone else had been. It *is* to do with wanting, and eroticism. I'd never experienced that. I remember we used to lie in this doorway at the back of Boots. Near the little park. He was a gas, because he had no fixed abode and I had to sit waiting for him while he had a bath in the public baths. He always bought Players Weights. Addicts always smoke Weights. It was charisma. The fact I'd drag him along to parties and say 'This is my boyfriend, he's a drug addict.' It was a real turn-on. It was like vicariously doing it myself. To me it was being dominated. Also it was a kick because it was so earthy. It was all this amazing London life he led. He really loved my body, really appreciated it. Yet he knew I was a virgin.

Anyway, back at school, the grammar-school boys came on a visit and I saw this guy and thought 'I've never seen you before.'

He was very attractive and had this kind of self-confidence that I liked, *and* he had a nice body. The way he walked and everything. I found out he was a friend of a friend and I told her I wanted a date. So he said to the friend, 'I want her but I can't,' because he thought she'd tell his mum and he'd get into trouble. I used to sit in the Wimpy Bar and stare at him. Of course we all had this terrible reputation for going down the Kavern. The myth was we slept with anyone.

It was Cathy McGowan days because I used to straighten my hair and I wore a red skinny-rib jumper and black corduroy skirt. I finally got this date with him, to meet him at 10 p.m. He was late and then he came striding round the corner. I looked up and smiled at him and said 'Curses, you've come. I was just thinking of all the nasty things I could call you.' We just kind of clicked. He smiled and put his arm round my shoulders. We walked down the High Street, up to the Wimpy Bar. I never, ever thought it would last and I put in my diary: 'You must appreciate it *now* because it's happening and it won't go on for ever.' I was in a rather double-bind situation because we used to have very risqué conversations about beds and things, but I never let him sleep with me because I was a virgin.

He claimed he was only going out with me because some father of another girl was after him. He always used to tell me how incredibly ugly I was and he'd say his friends couldn't understand what he was going out with me for. He'd say I had a great personality. As far as I was concerned he was very good looking. He had a beautiful body, he really spoiled me. He had very slim hips, and nice broad shoulders and chunky arms, not muscly but firm. He was very vain, and I found that attractive. And he had a big one. Really big. It still counts, I don't care what men say. I shall never forget that sensation. He used to get in a state and push it between my legs and say 'Please, please,' and I knew I'd have to tell him I was a virgin. So, at Christmas, I said I would sleep with him. It was at a party. I confessed I was a virgin and he was so pleased. We planned it as a birthday present but I'm afraid it happened before because you can't really control these things.

We used to sit in his parents' front room watching TV with the lights out. I learned everything from him. He brought out all my sexuality. I learned what it is to please a man. Up until then, I couldn't have encouraged a boy; it was more a question of warding them off, so I had never got into responding properly. He used to go on about what a fantastic body I had, how he was in love with my legs. He used to say I was incredible up to my neck! Awful, isn't it.

I suppose I didn't see much of you lot then because, quite frankly, all my energy went into him. We would watch TV. His mother would bring us a coffee and loudly cough in the corridor. In those days, things were a lot easier because you only had to take your knickers off, not take your tights down. So if someone came in, you only had to pull your skirt down with your knickers stuffed down the settee. In that sense, I'm still not used to getting into bed with no clothes on because I got accustomed to that state of deshabille.

GEORGINA Yes. I'm still like that. I prefer to keep my knickers on or something.

HEATHER I used to go round to his house in the holidays and get into bed with him in the morning.

POLLY Did you screw all the time?

HEATHER Yes. We used to go into the country, in fields, in people's gardens, in garages, even at dances we'd slip out into the dark.

POLLY Didn't you worry about it?

HEATHER I stopped associating sex with pregnancy. We used to do it all the way just before a period, at other times he'd come out. We used to meet before school in the morning – I was terribly wrapped up in him. He always acted out exaggerated relief when my period came. He told me he'd get an erection just looking at me. I worked out I never got pregnant through all my time with Tom because we used the withdrawal method and, really, because I always had to get up to walk home afterwards. Gravity was on my side. It all came out again! He knew about female orgasm. I remember he got quite cross with me if he felt I hadn't come. He told me once I didn't masturbate enough, that was why. So one day in the bath, I'd been thinking what on earth does one masturbate with – a candle, a banana, or what? I picked up the bathbrush and tried with the end of that! But it was horrid of course. All hard and cold. I mean I

71

wasn't experienced. I didn't need orgasm for the sake of it. I was turned on by Tom, not by a bathbrush.

It was bad for me, in one way. It let out all my sexuality and made sex so important. When I got to university a couple of years later, I got into this whole number with guys because I touched them up. I threatened them because I enjoyed it. I was made to feel guilty. So I had to play a game, much more coy than I was. I had to pretend to draw lines. I wasn't interested in all that groping around. I wasn't a virgin. Either you sleep with someone or you don't. I once went with this guy at a party. I quite fancied him and we got going. Because I'd had all this lovely sex, I knew enough to feel sorry for the guy if he was worked up and I didn't want to sleep with him, so I brought him off. I thought he'd be happy, but he said 'Why don't you go and make some other guy happy now?' I was the whore. I had a bad time in those days. And then I started finding out that other people weren't half as good. Tom and I kept going till half way through my second year at university. It was a tempestuous relationship.

On thinking about it, I can't stand that word screw, Polly. How can a word like that convey the passion, the incredible pull we felt for one another? We used to smile and say how lucky we were; we were on the inside, everyone else was on the outside. I've been listening to you lot raving on about hitching and Dylan, but that didn't stand out in my mind particularly. I realize I was totally wrapped up in him. I didn't need art or culture, or romantic heroes to excite my imagination and turn me on. We sparked off on one another. We had our own language and sense of humour. His friends were very shadowy to me; I didn't think much of them. And I know he didn't like mine. He used to loathe you, Polly, he thought you were pretentious and stupid. Just like you looked at him and dismissed him as a yob, because you never saw any of his depth. And in that way, I felt he has known me in a way that you, my close girl friends, will never know me. You can give yourself in such a total way to a man. That's what 'intimacy' is all about, that's why it's so precious and rare. It's taken me ten years to realize that it's the most important thing there is. Ten years of pursuing self-expression. Ha!

I know, you're thinking about all the times I cried, when he put me down. I knew deep down what I really believed. We survived so many bust-ups. I could meet him with a new girlfriend, and he'd lean forward when she went to the loo, and say: 'I want you back.' He could chat up a dozen other girls at a party and I knew he would come to me at the end, because what was between us was real, and so powerful.

OK, so it was illicit and that was a kick in itself. Do you know, we only spent the night together twice in two and a half years. I've always got a kick out of being a bit of a trail-blazer. Although I remember the first time being such an anti-climax that we solemnly decided to finish because we were incompatible. That didn't last long!

I did get a kick out of being the first of us to go all the way. At seventeen, you have that secret knowledge that you hope, provocatively, shows on your face, except when you get home of course! I used to get in and my mother would say: 'Your cheeks look very rosy. What have you been up to?' Not that she really wanted to know. As far as parents are concerned, ignorance is bliss. When she did find out she called me a prostitute and said no man would have me, although when she calmed down she said 'They needn't know,' in a conspiratorial tone. Those were the days men married virgins. I didn't care because I only wanted him. I didn't feel any guilt. How could it be wrong when it felt so right?

It was only later that I started wanting to taste other things. Part of the reason I blew it up in the end was because I didn't realize what I'd got. I thought every relationship would be like that. The other reason was fear, because he drove a wedge between me and my friends. Fear that he might one day leave me and I'd have nothing. That was the fear that drove me to escape him and come up to Manchester and you, Polly, betraying him, choosing my friends first. Part of the choice was because you also represented a dream, my fantasy self, everything I thought I would become, not knowing what lay ahead. Whereas with Tom it was all mapped out. We planned to travel, but somehow being with a man ties you down to a set identity. We did grow apart – well, we were apart so much after I went to university. I developed sides he'd never seen . . . that was how it cracked up. I've been looking for it ever since. Nothing less will do.

GEORGINA After Drew in Stratford, I went out with a grammar-school boy back home. But I knew too much about sex for school-boys after Drew. I went with this boy for social reasons; it meant I could claim to have a boyfriend and could go to parties at Christmas. With him, it was back to that whole number of hands up my jumper. At eighteen, I was getting quite bored by that. If only I could find someone to get into it with! I remember I couldn't be bothered to push his hands away – but he expected me to. In fact I could almost hear the tut-tut in his voice as he took his own hands off. I hadn't been with any local boys so I didn't have a bad reputation. I toyed with the idea of seducing him, but he was too nice for me. I remember I did the whole number on him, then felt guilty about getting rid of him.

Nothing much happened till the next summer – the one we all spent in Stratford. The big thing in my life, my first love, was that summer. Daniel – I remember him so clearly. He was an actor, up from London, to visit his friend for the weekend. He was incredibly beautiful – to me. Blond, English looking, medium height, medium build, with pale, fair skin – very effe-minate looking. very pretty, very deep. After a party, when everyone else had gone, we sank into a settee and it was the first time I'd enjoyed kissing so much. I mean that boy was beautiful. So kissing was beautiful, ecstatic, and a delight. I just adored him and adored his face. I can see it now – with his full, fruity grin and fruity voice, the slow eyes raised up, bright, funny, lovely – and beautiful cheekbones with full skin on the bone. I found all my latent energy and began to kiss his face myself and lick it. I loved the smell and taste of him. He said I was like a little dog.

We were having a party in a couple of weeks' time, so I in-vited him, never daring to believe he'd come. His friend said 'Oh Danny'll come if he makes it.' The rest of that scene is as vivid as a film. The night of the party, Polly and I went down to the Duck, didn't we? To get some male help. We walked in, bold as usual, and suddenly my heart started thumping. Daniel was there with a crowd at the bar. I was too overwhelmed with ex-citement. We went up to them, my hands all sweaty and I said calmly, 'Oh, hello, it's you.' He smiled one of his broad, slow smiles at me. I had to borrow some pennies, I was so nervous, and rushed to the phone to talk to you, didn't I, Carol?

The party was in some other girl's flat and he and I must have spent our night together there. That's the night I won't forget. I didn't lose my virginity, but I learned what skin against skin meant. I delighted in everything; I wanted more and more. He said things to me I loved, like 'You're a randy girl, you'll exhaust your husband in the first week'. Oh, but I worshipped him, then and all the following day. Then, of course, it was the next scene with him standing on the doorstep, as he shrugged, pecked me on the lips, and said 'See you.' I'd learned that boys wanted this show of freedom, liked the image of themselves wandering off into the unknown. He said 'You'll go through university and if you haven't found a husband by then, then you can worry.' Sexually, again I don't know what happened with Daniel. I don't remember his penis – so I don't know if I held it or not. He was very lazy; it was with him that I first lay on top of a man. He loved to lie back and have it done to him. I remember now, he said he'd had VD and so he couldn't screw for two years. There was no way he was going to rape me. But then maybe sex isn't like that for me. I think he may have kissed my cunt a little, not greedily, just gently. I know I just thought he was beautiful. He came to see me once at university and inevitably I'd moved on by then.

After six months at university, I'd spend the night with boys. I liked that. By then we'd got to the stage – I mean the boys had too – when they were quite prepared to do things to you with their hands but they didn't mind if you didn't want to go the whole way. I enjoyed spending the night with a boy, in a little single bed, all sticky and close. I never came off and I never brought them off. The next summer I fell in love and lost my virginity – so ended another chapter of my life.

POLLY Stratford! Oh yes. Desperate romantic fantasies for me, about one of the actors most of the time. Lying on that bed kissing *him* was like the high spot of the summer with his long legs wrapped round me, and me peering up into his spotty face. I thought he was beautiful.

GEORGINA Virginity was definitely our obsession that summer, wasn't it.

POLLY Hell, yes. Why each of us chose to lose it when we did I

75

don't know. I lost mine at university later that same year. We could trust those boys as they were going through the same number as we were. Why I never slept with any of those boys from the Kavern, Folkestone, St Ives or Stratford was because they weren't the same as us. It was too much to give in to them. They were either working-class lads wanting a screw or the actors up there, stars, and you don't get fucked by a star either. It had to happen at university. We were a family, brothers and sisters, that was safe. We knew and understood each other.

I went off for the night once, from that party in Stratford, with one of them. I was a bit drunk and God knows why I went because I knew it was dangerous. I knew this guy wasn't just fooling around for a quick snogging session. Some part of me feared it – I remember Ellie saying: 'Where the hell are you going with him?' He was the first guy I actually had oral sex with.

GEORGINA No? Good heavens! Before you'd lost your virginity? Oh, I suppose I did, too.

POLLY I remember lying on my back with this man's tongue up my fanny and I was thinking, like when I was four, 'There's no way I can get out of this. I've got to put up with it.' I couldn't actually say 'Get off, I don't want you to do this.' Still, there was a part of me liked it. Then he fell asleep. After a bit of eroticism, he crashed out. (*Howls of laughter*)

GEORGINA The saviour of we girls was the demon drink!

POLLY I didn't even leave then. But about 6 a.m. I crept out of bed, got dressed and ran back to our place. Then there was Simon. He was more talkable-to. That was probably the first prick I ever really looked at. You do a lot of groping in the dark without really looking. The two of us, naked, walked up the stairs and he had an erection. I remember the way it stood away from the body and I thought 'Isn't it strange.' He said 'You're a virgin, aren't you? Don't worry.' How could he put up with it?

HEATHER Well, it made a change for them too, didn't it? Anyway, what were they doing with girls like us?

POLLY He fell asleep, with his arms round me. And oh yes, I had Drew too – in the only way one did have him! It was frightening, a bit distasteful. His was big, wasn't it. But he was no threat either, was he. He wasn't going to actually penetrate me. I remember him bringing me back, and you looking at me,

Georgina, and when he went out the door you said 'I know what you've been doing.' I felt rather embarrassed.

One of my fears has always been of not being able to express my sexual demands because I'm not the French whore type: what I always see in other women – they're rounded, big-titted, rampant, very sexual and beautiful. I've often thought I really can't carry this off. I'm little, flat-chested and not beautiful. If I was Lawrence Durrell's Justine, I could. But how can you carry off all that passion if you're only little? They'd laugh at me and say 'You're not Sophia Loren.' But Drew taught me a lot, without being a threat to my virginity. He taught me a lot about what happens to pricks. I quite enjoyed that.

The part of the male body I find most erotic is just there, between the navel and the prick. They have such flat stomachs, and hair round their navel. I had a stage when I went off thin men, when I saw Alan Bates in *Women in Love*. I thought I'd try muscly men. But they never turned me on.

GEORGINA I like soft flesh there. Below the navel. Danny had soft skin and I could bury my nose in it. Gorgeous.

POLLY Oh no, I like it tight. (*screams of laughter*) What a desperate conversation! Shall we stop now and put dot, dot, dot? Actually I also remember sucking someone off when I was still a virgin.

GEORGINA Ridiculous, isn't it? You'd think it would be a much bigger barrier.

POLLY Again I had mixed feelings. I didn't really like doing it, but it pleased him so much. Then at university – some months later – there were some exciting men for the first time, of our own kind. The one I did it with in the end I chose because he was like the decadent actor types. Sexual ambivalence again. He was a very romantic man, you know. He quoted poetry and played the guitar. The night I went back to his room I went to a friend's room first and she said 'You're going to do it tonight, aren't you?' and I said: 'Yeah!' I knew it was the right time, and why not? He did use me a bit, in the end. He didn't follow it up.

The actual sex was boring! It hurt and it was boring. I remember thinking: 'Is this all it is?' I'd had much more fun beforehand. Like a prick up your arse, it was painful. Where's all the excitement, where's the desire? I did not have that desire I get now when you meet someone and you start sweating, your guts drop, and you're leaking – you just start melting. I still didn't know orgasm existed and I thought 'Is this all it is – what's the fuss about?' It was all right for them. They came. But it didn't mean a damn thing to me. The next morning, there was this blood. I was very pleased to have got rid of it, though. It was a great weight off my mind. I'd finally done it, thank Christ for that.

I told some girl I hardly knew that I'd lost my virginity. I had to tell someone. I felt very pleased with myself. Before that, it's a complete unknown. Then I slept around. It was all boring. Oh, there were seven of them until Ned – even Alan who I was so desperately in love with was boring – though perhaps if I'd been a little more sexually aware it might have been less so. With Ned I found that sex was exciting. He did actually get into other positions, other than lying on top of a woman. The first man who sat up or anything like that. Again orgasms did not come into it. One girl even gave me a lecture on getting a bad reputation. I used to feel in those days that I wanted to please men. If they were having a good time, then I could feel like a good sexy woman.

I don't see it as good now. What about my needs? I didn't know what they were or how to express them. All my sexual desire I pushed on to them. If they enjoyed fucking me, it meant I must be a sexually together girl. I always wanted to be – not promiscuous – but unshockable and decadent. I was into a very alluring, Mata Hari type pose – long black clothes and lots of eye make-up. If they were beautiful and seemed to want me, it was easy. I may set too much store by beauty. I can't imagine screwing someone slightly overweight and not beautiful. It's still only my idea of beauty, though. You wouldn't think half of them were beautiful.

Then I met Mick. I met him as part of the boozing crowd. I remember seeing this small, pretty person, a bit sulky, a bit moody, and my friend and I said 'Isn't he beautiful?' It was exam time and we used to sit in the revision room. I watched him over my Plato and thought 'Wow, I fancy you.' The first night we met, we went to a club and got pissed. I slowly got off with him. I turned on every bit of the flirtatious power I had. But when we got to the point I said 'no'. Mick got quite aggressive and said 'Trust a student to take all her clothes off and say "no".' He was very pissed anyway. I don't know why I refused to sleep with him that night.

HEATHER Fear of losing him, or of the old reputation perhaps?

POLLY I developed sexually with him, a lot, because we could explore. I had by then discovered the wonderful thing called orgasm. But I'd discovered it on my own. No *man* did it to me! And I only found out accidentally by masturbating. There must have been some unconscious hand guiding me saying 'Go on, see what's there.' I began to explore, and discovered it. Once I had, I loved it. Just rubbing my fingers on myself. I actually realized this is what sex is all about – there is something marvellous. I don't have vaginal orgasms now. I never have done by someone simply pushing in and out. It's still a problem for me. Do they exist separately, and I never let go enough to have them?

GEORGINA To me, it's not an outside feeling. It's very inside. It's a womb thing, hitting the neck of the womb. I have to consciously give way. I know what it's like to hold back. Difficult to say what it's like to hold back. Difficult to say what it is – not tension. It's allowing yourself to let go.

POLLY Yes, it's that control thing. I've been going into it a lot recently. There's a part of me loves and wants the penis thrusting in, and part of me hates it. That part of me doesn't want to be reduced to a shivering, shaking wreck. Women just fall apart, empty themselves. If anyone attacked you, you'd be finished. I cannot allow that aggressive male penis to reduce me to that. I will not be dominated like that and, at the moment, I resent it enough to say 'get off'. Not that I haven't enjoyed sleeping with people recently, but it's not for the orgasm side. I'm interested in the desire feelings, the penetration, the general physical erotica of skin and skin, touching, arms all round me, all that.

What I've always wanted in my life are major experiences. You know, Heathcliff and Cathy meeting over the hills, or that moment when you realize you've gone through some terrible misunderstandings with someone. And the same with orgasmic experience. All verging on religious experience. I fantasize the same scenes again and again. All those fantasies are much easier to handle than the reality. You see, sleeping with Mick got boring.

We were together three years. I think to sleep with someone over the years, and for it not to get boring, it has to be a numinous experience.

When I go to bed with a man now, I'm interested in his warm arms, in him as comfort and warmth, arms round you. Not in his prick. We all have that need for a mother too. Words like fucking, cunts, pricks, often make me squirm. I don't want to know about all that. It's distasteful. I do feel female and vulnerable. So the earthy part is harder for me. Men are more outward. If it moves, fuck it. I want my romantic, beautiful fantasy.

GEORGINA Oh, Polly, I didn't know you were such a romantic. It was easy for me meeting Dave like that. He was introduced to me by my room-mate at university. I was just getting worried I'd never meet anybody, that I wasn't normal. One evening I danced with Dave, and I remember he had a very funky way of dancing. He was young, middle-class, attractive, not in my adored way, but in that solid way – with a wide smile that reminded me of my uncle. We danced, we kissed, and suddenly I heard a sort of whoosh. He was making pleased noises. He whipped me round and said something like he knew I was going to be all right. He fell for me and I happily fell for him. By then I was nineteen and he was twenty-one. It was obvious we weren't going to just neck. I went back to his room, that first night, and we were properly involved, so we discussed sleeping together. But he had his Finals and so we agreed to wait till after that. I talked about it with my room-mate and I went to get the Pill. I was excited. I was lucky, I think. What was funny with him was that the first night I spent in his bed, I had a period. I was still using STs, I didn't dare use Tampax. So I kept my knickers on. He was horrified when he realized I had a smelly ST on. I did feel embarrassed. I only felt I understood my vagina after I'd lost my virginity.

We had a lovely, heady, painful time in bed together through those exams. I got so full of him I was literally sick. I threw up over the bed. When my room-mate was out one evening, he and I got into my little single bed and he put his hand up inside my cunt and there – for the first time ever – was a man who knew how to use his hand, and he actually brought me off. I just knew that for once I'd let go and reached a peak, and he said something

I never forgot. 'There, you've had two more than the majority of women in this country have ever had in their lives.' Because I'd come three times. I said 'What?' And he said 'Orgasms.' The whole debate had only just started in public, but I didn't know anything about it.

Things had already begun to go wrong with him before I actually lost my virginity, though. I remember looking out of the window one day thinking 'Oh, please God let it happen.' We'd begun to bicker. He used to put me down. He'd been hurt by a previous girl and I thought he hated me when he compared the two of us. I'd go like a moody and defensive eighteen-year-old. I can still be. That's what I've done with Martin just recently. But I remember telling myself to play it cool till the virginity thing was over. I couldn't let this opportunity go.

We gave a party after the exams. We had a flat by then, my room-mate and I. In the night, or the morning after the party, that's when we actually did it. Of course it wasn't very exciting. Hard, painful, no blood for me, and mildly disappointing. But I knew to expect that, and that future times would be better. We had fine times together, though he insisted I call it fucking, not making love. He couldn't bear female sloppiness. It finished with him a few weeks later. I was too selfish. Or maybe it was just I didn't want him as a partner in life. He was more a notch on my experience belt.

5 God said 'Give them the Pill'

You went to the finest school, Miss Lonely . . .
Nobody's ever taught you how to live out on the streets,
  and now you're gonna have to get used to it.

How does it feel? To be on your own, with no direction to go?
  Like a complete unknown, like a rolling stone?

'Like a rolling stone' seemed to be Bob Dylan's message to nice bourgeois girls desperate to get out. We sat in my bedroom, half a dozen girls who'd come through the grammar-school mill, and Dylan's song had a powerful effect. Creating that feeling of independence, of wanting to fly like a bird. Now it was time to leave home. We were eighteen coming up nineteen. It was time to show what mettle we were made of. Heather, Georgina, Mag and I were going to universities. Polly and Ellie were left out though.

POLLY I didn't get the 'A' Levels. I got sick in my stomach and couldn't cope with the exams. Yet it was me who'd made the others want to go to university. My father came to visit me while I was staying with Georgina that summer. He was very cross with me because I was still saying I was going to be an actress. He didn't really know what he wanted me to do – other than go to university and be a teacher. That was what you did in my family. They wanted me to be like them. So any spark was squashed. There was also the middle-class, puritan ethic which says 'Thou shalt be humble, hard working and get your head down'! I hadn't even been allowed to go to art school because they said it was a waste of time – just the Saturday morning one that Heather went to. I agreed in the end to retake my 'A' Levels if I could join the others at Manchester where they were at university. My father kept pointing to Georgina as a good example of what a young woman was meant to be like.

GEORGINA While Polly's father was talking, I remember looking out of the window, feeling embarrassed, wondering what sort of future we were all going to have. This was the moment of departure. Mag's older sister seemed to have gone one way. She had been very clever at school, had gone to university and was brilliant there too. She came over to me as the sort of wise, mature and interesting woman – a bit of the bluestocking – but she lacked the raunchy quality we felt we had as well. She was the new kind of career woman, I suppose. Feeling that I was the most academic of the bunch, I thought perhaps that had to be my way too. But I didn't really fancy it. It wasn't so much the phrase 'career woman' that got me by then, but the whole prospect seemed lifeless and dull. Mag's sister threw us a week or so later when she came on a visit and announced that she was six months pregnant. She'd done it deliberately by a man she loved but could never marry. How romantic! She'd taken that other step, headed straight for single parenthood. We were amazed. Not really envious. We agreed that if it'd been us we'd have gone all out to get the man we loved rather than his baby! There really were very few patterns of life for us to look up to. Whose example were we to follow? Look at what happened to Ellie . . .

She had not run away to university. She was not so sure of what she was going to do after a couple of years at the local art school. She wrote to me once when I was safely ensconced in student life, that we were lucky as at least we felt secure for the next three or four years. She had no framework for her life. Ellie met Derek just then. She went off to a different art college but gave it up after a few weeks and went to live with Derek in London. She took clerical jobs. They lived together for about six months before she got pregnant. She never thought about abortion. You didn't in those days, in her kind of environment. She thought about having the baby and having it adopted, but in the end they just drifted along and got married when she was five months pregnant. I remember she wrote saying it would be rather nice to get married young and have a baby: 'I know that none of you lot would do something like this at nineteen, but then I'm not secure enough to want adventures like you. I've always wanted brothers and sisters, being an only child, and conventional family life. So maybe the best thing is to create it for myself.'

Ellie's wedding was an important day for me. I *hated* the thought of it. To me she was copping out, giving up, writing off her life and her youth. I wrote back that she mustn't do it. Derek must have thought me a real interfering so and so. To me none of it really fitted with her semi-bohemian image. She refused a proper wedding though, refused to wear a hat or carry a matching handbag! Ellie always had been nature's child. I was one of their witnesses. We tried to laugh together at the cliché of her being five months pregnant. As she was a thin, angular sort of girl, it didn't really show. On the group wedding photos, I thought she and Derek looked like a couple of children, trying to put on a bold face as they struggled through this particular jungle. But when they drove off in their car, to go on honeymoon, I felt quite envious.

We talked about it recently, did Ellie and I. She and Derek

are still together. Quite happy. They've got three girls: the eldest is ten. Neither Heather, Polly or I have any children. Ellie said, 'I was too young at nineteen. It's too young for anyone to know their own mind. If it's worked out it's by luck rather than because it was a good thing. Though I think one of my big factors was always not to be like my mother, which is why I went on hastily and had three children. I always thought of her as being particularly career-minded. She's quite successful, having come from a poor background and pushed her way forward. But I didn't want to be like that. If I hadn't got pregnant, I suppose I would have gone to training college and done art. But I don't see that life would have been any better, do you? It all started off very badly, the marriage. I'm amazed when I look back and think how trapped I was in London with a baby, knowing no one. Suzy and I were very dependent on each other for the first two years of her life. Then I had Anna and we moved to Kent. It was better for me on that housing estate, because everyone had children. It was a very ordered way of life. I don't feel I missed out on my youth. There's no point in thinking that way anyway. It seems when I talk to you that it'd only be a question of exchanging one sort of hell for another'.

POLLY Once Ellie was pregnant there was a world of difference between her life and ours. The reason for it lies in her line, 'I wasn't secure enough to want adventures.'

GEORGINA We grew up assuming we could have our freedom and adventures, and come out unscathed, didn't we? Maybe we seem cold and heartless to other women. One thing we were sure of. Now was the time to say goodbye to provincial, small-town life. That same summer, before we left home, I remember looking out of my bedroom window (we lived in a flat in the town) down into the office next door. I would stare at the girl sitting in there typing. She had been at school with us. Not one of our circle of friends but a bright girl who had gone through 'A' Levels, in the same way. Now she sat tamely at her desk and typewriter. She had sandwiches in front of her and – it's a big 'And' – a Diamond Ring glittering in the sunlight on her left hand! She was engaged, she was going to be married. Her life now meant being in a good secure job, eating sandwiches to save for the mortgage, and looking adoringly into her loved one's eyes. I didn't want to know about all that kind of thing!

HEATHER The idea of being trapped there in that town! . . . having babies meant settling down, doing what the man expected of you . . . that was really not what I was after in life, although I was still totally involved with Tom. I remember once we thought I was pregnant and he looked so happy, making out he was rocking a baby, but I had nightmares.

GEORGINA We took the warnings about the dreaded trap very seriously. We all read Edna O'Brien's *A Girl With Green Eyes* and *Girls In Their Married Bliss*. 'The book can be read,' Edna O'Brien said, 'as a cold early morning signal to young girls – don't rush into marriage.' None of us could really believe Ellie had done such a thing. She'd broken faith. There was another book, I remember, which greatly influenced me at the time. It was called *Enough Rope*, by Andrea Newman, and it was serialized in *Honey*. Ellie and I both read it, before she got pregnant this was. It put its finger on the nub of our anxieties. Valerie, in the novel, was about to go to university. But she had fallen for a very attractive, not so clever, rather glamorous guy. She enjoyed zooming round in his sports car, but ended up getting pregnant and so could not go to university. People maybe don't realize what a big adventure that was for our generation of girls – what a perfect way out of the trap that women in the past had always fallen into. Valerie's rope of freedom, though, had been enough to hang herself on. Getting pregnant was falling into the old trap. It would mean, as happened later to Ellie, that the man would say 'Let's get married,' and then you have to curb all that enthusiasm for life, all that energy, and settle down to cooking meals and washing nappies. I felt very strongly for Valerie's fate. In 1965, it was pre-Pill days for unmarried girls. Pre-sex-education too. Valerie had been warned, she said, about his desire. But what no-one had ever warned her of was her own desire – which would be just as uncontrollable, just as dangerous.

I wrote it all down in my notebook at the time, the bits that moved me. Marianne (her friend) said to Valerie, 'You're not in love with him are you Val?' 'No.' 'Not at all?' 'No, we've had a lot of fun, going to places, and he's terribly attractive. I'm quite fond of him in a way, or was, till this happened.' Marianne says, 'It's as though you were the wrong way round . . . It's like you were the boy and he was the girl. I mean in your feelings about each other.' Val: 'I've got to get there (university), I can't let this ruin my life. People do go away and have babies and have them adopted and nobody ever finds out . . .' 'You want a superman.' 'Yes, I do. You're quite right. It's possible; people do it. My mother did it. That's what I want.'

None of us wanted to get pregnant. We wanted to be free. To live life. Then the magic drug came along just at the right time. Before I went away to university I had, of course, heard about the Pill. I'd even taken it for a while to help me get through my exams, but I didn't know how to get hold of it as contraception. Unmarried girls weren't allowed the Pill then. We just read about it in odd newspaper articles. Girls' magazines did not write about contraception in those days.

ME There was one newspaper article which missed our notice though, a story reported on 7 September 1965 under the heading, 'Mystery of Birth Pill Wife's Death':

The death of a healthy young wife six months after she had started taking birth control pills raised the question again yesterday – Can they be killers? Cynthia Leigh, aged 22, died from thrombosis, something very rare in young people, especially for it to come out of the blue without an underlying cause is almost unheard of.

She died, but no-one wanted to listen in those days to any warnings. Word had gone round among the girls. The Pill had something to offer we all wanted. Safety in sexual freedom.

GEORGINA I can say quite proudly and honestly that I did not consider losing my virginity till my method of contraception was sorted out. As I tended to see babies as a trap, it is not very surprising. Yet it gave me a great kick to feel so contemporary. I was helped by the fact that my flat-mate in the first year at university was a year older, from London, and more sophisticated about life and love than us lot. She brought the news of the Pill to Manchester. There were times I thought she was over-doing the emancipated woman angle. I wasn't going to get the Pill to be ready for when *it* might happen. But, even so, she was the kind of girl who luckily had her ear to the ground. She knew what to do.

In 1965 the Student Health Centre would not prescribe the Pill. The Brook Clinic, or the Family Planning, would not prescribe the Pill to unmarried girls. There was one doctor, a retired woman, in Manchester who decided she preferred to prescribe the Pill to girl students than see them get pregnant. She was a real pioneer. She had a red brick house in the suburbs. When I met Dave, fell in love, and we agreed we wanted to sleep together, it was then I asked my girlfriend what to do. Dave agreed to wait for me. She and I took a bus trip, me clutching two grubby pound notes, to see the lady doctor. I was questioned closely about my relationship, which was still very new. You had to say you were going to get married after you'd both graduated! I learned to fantasize a bit then about Dave. You always do for family planning doctors.

What I really wanted to tell her was, 'Look, this is a very exciting day. Here am I making a conscious decision to lose my virginity, because I'm crazy about him. And I feel really randy and I'm desperate to lose it. I don't care whether he and I get married so much as when he and I are going to be able to get it off together. And I'm getting an extra kick out of the fact I'm taking control over my own body, being responsible, and no, I don't equate sex with babies.' She gave me the tablets – Gynovular 21 they were – a packet of little pink pills with the days written above them, which I never really enjoyed swallowing because they made me feel slightly sick. I took them for the correct two weeks before I lost my virginity. I felt very emancipated. This was what being a woman meant to me!

Looking back, we were a strange new breed of women. Eating the first fruits of what was really Eve's apple. Sexual licence. Licence to screw without getting pregnant. The Pill brought about *the* biggest change in women's lives. Within a year, the stiff medical establishment had softened. The local family planning clinic had an unmarried girls' night once a week. The Student Health Centre still kept out of it, though within a couple of years all students knew that their doctors gave girls the Pill and boys Valium, whatever the problem!

POLLY I never thought about contraception. When I was nineteen and twenty, my mind was a complete blank about it. Despite the fact I used to sleep around until I met Mick. All that year I was screwing everyone. Why I didn't use anything I can't understand to this day. I read through my 1967 diary the other day. There were all these people I was getting off with and yet every month I wrote, 'Thank God I'm not pregnant.' I remember being very impressed when you got the Pill, Georgina. By the time I'd got it together to go for the Pill, I was pregnant but didn't realize.

Mick was younger than me, only seventeen, but he was my first long-term relationship. So it was then I felt I must get myself protected. It was the summer holidays and Heather and I went to Eastbourne to work in a factory. We were on the night shift and I felt sick the whole time but I put it down to the fact my body was on a changed rhythm. When I was a few days late I took Primodos. Nothing happened. That meant I was ten days late as I'd had a period the month before. In fact I was a month more pregnant than that. I've had no faith in periods ever since! It had been a reasonable one too.

ME I didn't last long, did I? So much for emancipation and freedom to screw. I was almost first in and first out of the game. I soon became cynical. It was just before Christmas in 1969 and I was going to stay with my American boyfriend's family in New York. I was incredibly excited, though panicking at the problems I had, fixing up a charter flight on my own from a Manchester flat with no phone. I'd just left university and started work. I'd been on and off the Pill for a couple of years. I was sharing a flat in Manchester with a girlfriend. We had to run for a bus one day and she left me standing, breathless and panting. A week later, in the night, I suddenly felt I was about to choke. I coughed and brought up this sweet sickly stuff which spilled on to a hanky I grabbed hold of in the dark. In the morning I stared with horror at the bright red blood staining the tissue. I knew about Keats and Shelley! I threw it away feeling embarrassed. I told Heather about it and we both agreed it must have been a nosebleed in the night. I pushed it out of my mind. Three days later, in the afternoon, I had a pain behind my right breast. But I was involved in the excitement of going away, saying goodbye to Polly and Mick, to Georgina and Heather and I made a joke of it. It went away in the end. But at work, that evening, one of the guys there I'd told the story to, was around to see it happen again. I choked, gagged, and coughed a quantity of blood again. My instinct was again to hide it. I was going away the day after next after all.

He got me to a doctor there and then. That evening was spent having lots of X-rays and tests. I was sent back to our flat, where I told Heather what was going on. I took my Pill that night as usual – I was going to see my boyfriend soon, wasn't I? The next morning, feeling bright and optimistic, I skipped into the doctor's surgery to be told not to run around, to sit down while he broke the news to me. I was to cancel my flight, because the X-rays showed I had an inflamed heart. It was the winter of the big flu epidemic. I was to go back to my parents' home, and not stand around in draughts. Extraordinary news for someone like me. None of it made sense. The doctor had not guessed even then, which just showed me later how little the medical profession knew.

The first clue I had of what might be going on was when I telephoned my boyfriend and heard his worried voice say, 'You're not taking the Pill still? and I said I was. 'Stop it immediately, it's the Pill. One of my friends here has just spent hundreds of dollars having thromboses taken out of her legs.' Thrombosis? It was the first I'd heard of it. Flashback to a couple of weeks before when Polly had come round to visit. We'd both read articles of the possible dangers of the Pill, but it was to do with cancer, and wouldn't affect us till our forties. It didn't seem a threat at twenty-two. We stood on the doorstep, as she was about to leave, and I said to her, 'We'll face that problem when it comes. I'd rather live now and pay later than not be able to live at all.' And we both laughed, confident that we were right.

It was the specialist who listened to my story, asked my parents to leave the room, and then asked if I was taking the Pill. He told me he was sure it was the Pill, that he was extremely concerned about it. He said it was very rare for someone of my age to have a pulmonary embolism with no other warning. He explained how lucky I had been. That if the wandering clot had caught me in the heart or brain, 'I'd have been out like a light.'

He then asked me if my parents knew I was taking the Pill. I said 'no', looking worried. He promised not to tell them if that was what I wanted. I said 'Oh please don't,' which was a bad decision. But in those days young girls didn't let on to their parents.

In hospital I lay in bed, bored, looking out of the window, taking my quarter-tablet of rat poison, Warfarin, having my blood tested every day so I end up with a junkie's arm, and I remember thinking 'What price emancipation now?' I felt very bitter and angry that in all the talk about the Pill, in all the propaganda about sexual freedom for girls, no-one had ever warned me it might come to this. I'd never been told I could not have my cake and eat it. The guy might have free sex. But I was paying for it, not him. I never had an easy time with contraception after that.

POLLY I was on the Pill altogether for about seven years with a few months off here and there. I never had any trouble with it, no weight gain, no nausea. In fact, I had less periods and life was easy. Spontaneous sex was possible when I wanted. But I went off the Pill in the end, because when there was no man around, I had this thing about 'What am I taking this for? There's no regular man in my life.' Also I felt if I could stop smoking and come off the Pill, I wouldn't worry about my health. You had been ill from the Pill and I was very aware of that other dreadful story of another girl we knew from Burton who had died after giving birth because of the Pill. Also I was into my freak culture and interest in living naturally by then. I went to the Marie Stopes to get a cap, but when I stopped taking the Pill I didn't have periods for eight months. Then, when I went back to the clinic to ask for a Copper 7, the doctor said I had scar tissue after my abortion and couldn't have one. I felt doomed to the cap for ever. In the end, I went to see a lady gynaecologist and she was marvellous. She was aware that contraception is to do with emotions and another person and love. I'd never come across that from any other medical person. Now, I wouldn't want the coil anyway, because I don't want to take any more risks with my uterus or my fertility. My sex life suffers. But I don't really care at the moment. Though, of course, with passing lovers the cap *is* a drag.

GEORGINA The creams ruin sex, don't they.

POLLY Creams? Oh, I haven't bothered with all that stuff for two years now.

GEORGINA You're crazy.

POLLY You know, I long now for the days when I needn't worry. Because one level of sex has to be making babies, and that must be nice. I've never done that.

HEATHER I never used any contraception all that time with Tom. We used the rhythm method topped up with withdrawal, which was why my mother found white stains on my school mac and I had all the screaming rows with her. She called me a whore. When I did get pregnant, and I went to the doctor to say I was overdue, I was too embarrassed to mention the fact we'd used the withdrawal method.

Tom and I had a row that Easter and I went off with someone else. That was the first time I was sleeping with someone who I wouldn't want to marry, so I realized I had to be more careful. Mind you, the guy was a virgin and wasn't much danger! But I went along to a private health clinic in Manchester because if you weren't married you couldn't get contraception. It cost me twelve guineas in those days! I remember feeling really humiliated because it seemed so dirty. I had to take off my clothes, lie on the operating table, and he kept feeling my breasts for ages, and had his hand up me for a long time saying I was deceptive in my size for a cap. Another year passed and I finished with Tom. Polly and I went off to Eastbourne and I didn't take the cap with me because I wasn't expecting to sleep with anybody. But we met some silly American and went up to London, where I met Robin and spent the weekend with him. We went off to the country to screw, but it was already fading for me. We had a very unsatisfactory screw. He was meant to be withdrawing. I couldn't believe it later that I was pregnant from something so short and unsatisfactory. Sod's Law I call it.

That summer in Eastbourne, Polly was all over the moon for Mick but kept lying in bed saying she felt sick. I thought she was just being pathetic because we were working nights. Polly had had a period but eventually saw a doctor who advised her to act quickly if she 'wanted to do anything'. He couldn't mention abortion. I'd had a period too. Mine were never more than three days and I suppose it only lasted a day. I stayed on in Eastbourne after Polly raced back to Manchester. I shared a flat with some university students from Brighton. I didn't fancy Robin at all by then. When I missed my period, I also began to wake up late in the mornings feeling sick. But still I didn't think I was pregnant. I went back to Manchester because I was going on holiday with a friend, Annie. The doctor's letter followed me up there, saying, 'Dear Heather, This is conclusive proof that you are pregnant.' That was it. Not one word of advice or help, from the family doctor too. I couldn't bear the thought of Annie's disappointment, she was really good and helped me. As it happens she was pregnant too that summer, she just didn't know it then! That was the summer we all got pregnant.

I went on the Pill after the abortion. I remember in Manchester, the next year, a guy said to me it was immoral to be taking the Pill and not be sleeping with anyone. I said 'After what I've just been through I'm not taking any more chances.' I put on weight and got a bit depressed. The doctor said it disagreed with me, that I should go back to the cap. But I changed doctors instead. I went to that same woman in Manchester as you, Georgina. That's when I first began to fictionalize my boyfriends too, because that's what she wanted to hear. You run them all into the same one.

When I first went off the Pill, two years later, I didn't have a period for four months. I was a bit concerned but they told me it was 'normal'. Huh! I carried on, off and on, altogether for six years. Then I had a Copper 7 put in, which my body rejected twice. So they tried their new experiment on me, the T. Coil. That was fine, except my periods stopped completely. When I told the doctor the reason, why I hadn't filled in the 'bleeding' squares on the chart I was keeping for his control study, he got really angry. He told me I was neurotic, that it was all only emotional. Of course ovulation and contraception are linked with the emotions. What does he think sex is all about? I haven't had proper periods since. An acupuncturist brought them back once. When I'm sleeping with someone regularly I get a bleed for a day every five or so weeks. But my cycle is right out.

After years of patronizing nonsense from doctors, telling me I was neurotic, I got myself to a sympathetic female gynaecologist who actually had me in hospital for hormone tests. There I was, in my thirtieth year, sitting in a hospital bed having one doctor test my imbalanced hormones, while across London another doctor, so smug and smart, was handing out his famous T. Coil. I feel bitter and angry, but more than that, sad. Perhaps I should have had my babies the times I've been pregnant. I'm scared stiff it's too late now.

6 Dear dad, please send a crate of gin

Yet back in the summer of 1965, just before leaving home to go to university, it seemed as if we could cope with everything. We even had a joke between ourselves about what we would do if we did get pregnant. It was a line from a letter you would write home from university, like the ones kids send from camp. It opened, 'Dear dad, please send a crate of gin,' and just added as an afterthought, '—and say I'm sorry to mother.' It could make you cry if you think about it now. What we didn't know then was that all that freedom brought a lot of problems with it.

GEORGINA Contradictions and paradoxes I call them. Think about the mini-skirt. The worst thing about the mini was it made you look like a little toy girl, just there to please men. Guys used to call us 'chicks' and 'birds' which I always hated. I'll never forget how angry I was when I swung through the students' union to hear someone refer to me as a dolly bird. But then I'm still the same paradox. I want to please men, I want to be fancied and liked, and yet I don't want to be seen as the kind of girl who lives only for men.

But mini-dresses in hot summer weather were quite something. I know boys used to laugh on the first day of warm weather as they said the girls were coming out in their flowery knickers. I enjoyed the 'flasher' feeling. I used to drag my bicycle out of the shed, enjoying watching bus conductors stare as I wiggled by. I loved wearing those short, revealing dresses. I loved the kick of watching their effect on men, of sending out those sexual vibes.

It got worse when the next year we stopped wearing bras. It was nothing to do with the Women's Movement as I remember it, but more to do with wanting to flaunt ourselves. Your nipples show, your breasts, even if they're little, swing and move so anyone can see them. And under cotton T-shirts that gives *you* a nice feeling.

HEATHER I never could go without a bra; I was too big. It made us big-breasted girls feel even more uncomfortable. I liked mini-skirts though, because I've got good legs.

POLLY I don't remember anything about mini-skirts except they crept up the leg. I went to Canada in a not very short mini-skirt. The expatriates were all saying 'We love your short skirts and long hair,' and the redneck cowboys were saying 'Dirty hippies!' When they stared at me as I walked by, I felt vaguely threatened but also vaguely excited, I think. Everyone got into it, that was all – I must have looked a funny shape, being so small. It was ages before I stopped wearing a bra, too. All the time I was a student I wore one. I'd been at work a year and then it was a sophisticated girl from London who hadn't worn a bra in years who inspired me to stop. I had got into the 'natural' shape bras by then. Before that I used to wear boned ones that gave me a nice little figure. When I went without a bra, I just dropped. Being quite flat-chested I had to get into a new kind of sexiness. You know, a sort of boyish sensuality. I had to make myself look completely flat, with just little nipples sticking out. You have to make something of it, wear tight body-fitting little T-shirts, arch your back, and offer the hint of a shape – and never hunch your shoulders. I was always self-conscious though, because I am small – yet my breasts still bounce around.

GEORGINA I've a very vivid memory of one summer, feeling good, wearing my shorter than short dress, and my hair long. I met a very sexy man who was older and more experienced. He invited me round to his house. I turned up feeling very summery and sexy. It was there, though, when I took off my short dress for him, let it drop (remember my scene from *A Town Like Alice* I'd loved as an adolescent), and revealed myself without a bra, knowing I was on the Pill, and he expected me to be so, that I had the feeling there was no pretence any more. No games to be played. No way I could say 'be careful with me,' or 'watch out for my emotions,' or worry if I get pregnant, or think of my honour, or that my parents wouldn't like it.

I'd offered myself as free. Taking off that dress and revealing myself naked meant there was nothing to cover myself with, no way to hide. I had some of the best sex of my young life. But at nineteen, or twenty, I felt it was tougher for me than him. I was throwing away centuries of breeding, of manners and customs for women. I was putting myself in the role of the debased woman but I was also saying 'I'm not debased, my currency is as strong as yours.' You have to fight your psyche hard not to weaken sometimes.

All I did was, as usual, convince myself I wanted him to marry me. Then I got very upset when, of course, he didn't want that. It's all water under the bridge now. But in two short years, the climate had changed so radically. From wondering how to get the Pill in 1965, there was I in 1967 being used by a man who just expected I'd be on the Pill, who just took it for granted. I remember in March 1967, *Honey* ran their first feature on 'Birth control and the single girl'. I cut it out. Abortion did not become legal till later in 1967; contraception did not get publicized till that year. Right now, it is still only ten years exactly from the beginning of that kind of freedom – which is a startling thought.

HEATHER Of course it was 1967, but before the Act, when I was first pregnant. I'd thought I was pregnant the summer before, and I did actually drink gin in a hot bath that time! That makes you feel really terrible. That evening I told Annie, she and I immediately worked out what to do. I went down to London and cashed in all my travel tickets and foreign money. Then we went tramping round the Harley Street doctors. We'd been given the addresses of sympathetic doctors by Polly's sister. It was obvious what I was there for. Then I'd be asked, 'Do you have a doctor's note?' and was turned away. At one of them, though, I saw this man's face peering out of the window at me. 'Is it urgent?' he said. He charged me ten guineas for a letter of introduction to a woman whose surgery he shared! He told me to go and get a letter from a psychiatrist saying I was not fit to have a baby. That cost another ten guineas. Annie came with me as we trailed off to the psychiatrist who was 80 and deaf. Have you ever tried convincing someone who is deaf that you're depressed?

I just thought 'Let me get rid of this and I'll never be depressed again!'

In the meantime, I'd rung up Robin and summoned him. He, poor guy, thought I was going to have him back. I gave him the letter to read. Never for a moment had I thought of having the baby. I knew it would ruin my university career and I didn't want a child because it wasn't Tom's. I just wanted to get this parasite out of me. I was really desperate, literally ready to commit suicide. I said to Robin, 'Can't you sell your scooter?' and he said 'No.'

I had to go out to the woman doctor's that evening. She kept me sitting in the hall while she ate her dinner. It was a house full of beautiful paintings and Persian rugs. I was thinking 'Am I the next Persian rug?' She told me I was two and a half months. She would book me in for next week and it would be one hundred and fifty guineas. 'Where the fuck am I going to get one hundred and fifty guineas?' I thought. She said '—and they want it in cash.' I went back to that flat in Eastbourne where the Brighton boys were staying. They found an American woman photographer, willing to lend me a hundred pounds. She had a flat in Camden Town. Annie and I could stay with her. I rang Robin and he'd told his parents. His mother came to the phone and started cross-examining me about whether it was his! I was hysterical and Annie had to take over for me. They came up to London. His mother met me and went on about me seducing her flaming son. She said 'I always find it best to keep that bit of mystery in reserve.' And I said 'I don't use my body to bribe people.' Robin had arranged for his parents to give me eighty pounds. They left it in a post office for me to collect. I was so bitter. I paid my half out of my twenty-first birthday-present money I was getting. His parents paid his.

My mother, unfortunately, read a letter from a friend and we had another of our huge rows. But my parents never offered to help. Anyway the abortion was wonderful. I was in this nice clinic for three days, being pampered. The doctor said 'Don't drink, and don't let me see you again.' I felt so good, so relieved. I rushed back to Eastbourne to a twenty-first birthday party, determined nothing worse could ever happen to me!

POLLY Remember I was in Eastbourne thinking I was ten days

overdue? Well, when I got back to Manchester, I guessed I was two or three weeks over, though I had to look in my diary because Mick and I had hardly seen each other. There was a great gap between the end of term and one quote in my diary which said 'We almost made it!' I didn't think it had been sufficient to get pregnant by. And the reason we didn't do it properly that time was because we were waiting for me to have a period so I could go on the Pill. I had the tablets all ready and waiting. Mick was marvellous. I had begun to get more and more anxious before I saw him. In my diary I wrote 'I must never tell him,' because we'd both failed our exams and I didn't want it to look as if I'd trapped him. When I did tell him, he said, 'It'll be all right.' It's funny, from the beginning it was clear to Mick and me that we weren't having a child, we were having an abortion.

Heather had just had her private abortion. Ellie had got pregnant, married and had the baby. But because of my sister in London I knew how to go about things. I was lucky though. I had a guy who wanted to stay with me, a sister, a brother, and a psychiatrist who all supported me. It was 1967, still before the Act, but I got a National Health abortion for free. But I ended up with a dreadful consultant.

I just had not thought of having children in any realistic way. Mick and I had just met, it was the beginning of our university careers and of our relationship. The parallel was Ellie, and I didn't want that at nineteen. I wanted to get famous and have adventures. There was no doubt in my mind. We never sat down for a moment and said 'Right, do we want to keep this?' I never said 'I'm sad about it.' Nor did I suffer a sense of loss or from depression, although I do feel kind of guilty about it now. The child was an intrusion on our great love and our great relationship. We did all that justification thing, of course – about it being just as much a sin to bring an unwanted child into the world.

Anyway, the doctor told me I was four weeks more pregnant than I thought. I sat bolt upright and said 'Oh no I'm not.' He said 'Don't argue with me.' Then he pronounced this terrible fate – a Caesarean section. 'That is how I do abortions,' he said. By now I was trying to hold back the tears and the terror. I said I'd go and think about it. Mick was waiting for me and I howled and complained to everyone I knew. I was terrified at the idea of a major operation. I still feel mistrustful of the whole episode. I don't know why he did it that way. He addressed one of the registrars too, saying 'Her uterus is rather set back.' For ever after I've blamed my lack of vaginal orgasm on my uterus being set back! But it was either that or find one hundred and fifty pounds. I had no choice. In I went.

It was, in fact, a very important and powerful experience. The night before I went in, Mick got pissed and sick, so I had to go to the hospital on my own, carrying my little bag. An Irish woman said to me 'I'm in for a hysterectomy,' and I said 'I'm in for an abortion.' From then on we became great buddies and helped each other through. I could talk to her about all sorts. She was Irish and had had ten children. I used to talk to her about living with Mick, and about sex before marriage. There was an intimacy also between the whole ward. There were some middle-class housewives, learning their amateur drama scripts, in for a scrape, some screaming miscarriages in the night, uptight girls in for abortions who wouldn't talk, and one amazing night-club singer who'd had nine abortions. She was tough, but the life and soul of the ward.

The operation was extraordinary because I didn't feel ill, just pain from the stitches. Poor Mick came twice a day all the way through it. It was then he said 'We'll go away next summer,' and that clinched us. We had a relationship that would last. I only wanted *him* to visit me after that. It was all completely untraumatic. After the fortnight, I came out. My breasts swelled to be enormous for me and I had to take tablets. I did feel weepy but it was good to get home, to be with Mick and out of hospital.

Whatever my feelings were, I repressed them. The first night out of hospital I was down the bar with my mates patting me on the head saying 'Here's a drink', and the doctor had said 'Don't dance, take the Pill, and don't come back.' I got back into the swing of life. There was no grief, nothing. It all sounds very cold. Mick probably felt worse than me. He looked helpless and inadequate. It was a shared responsibility.

I've never really thought about the abortion. Yet I have the constant reminder of the five-inch scar. Perhaps there is a lot of pain in there? I get flashes of it when I think that child would be nine or ten now. I tried to imagine it but couldn't give it a sex or a name. I feel very frightened of getting pregnant by accident again because I couldn't have another abortion now. Now that I'm thirty, and I'm alone, there is a terrible nagging thing that says 'Was that your only chance?' Rationally you know you can get pregnant, but my guilt comes out that way. I see it as the punishment due to me.

HEATHER Yes, my ideas have changed tremendously, too. I had the second abortion five years later. Again I had an abortion because I was in a situation where a relationship had died and I did not want, this time, Benny's child. I'd had such a good thing with Benny, the guy from the fairgrounds, and then it had gone awful. Typical of me. I went off the Pill because it was all over. Then he comes back one night and I slept with him to make him go away quietly, and I get pregnant. I realized I'd boobed. I'd no financial resources. I didn't want to bring the child up on my own. To have that child say 'Why?' to me one day. I was lucky. I got a National Health one. But I feel, now, that abortion is murder and I think I've faced the responsibility of it. I've changed spiritually. It all began that summer I went travelling with Benny, anyway. That's when my different outlook on life began. It was after that I got into astrology; that I dropped out of my straight teaching job. But when the second abortion came . . . no, I don't want to talk about it. I mean I'd made a real mess of my life at that point. *I'd* become the patient, the mess, the victim. You don't really want to dredge all that up, do you? I spent a long time feeling really bad. That's when I re-erected all my values; realized that although abortion can be the best solution in a bad situation, it doesn't absolve you.

The simple fact is if I hadn't had my abortions, I'd have a child of five and a child of ten with me now; living, real people. I don't get morbidly obsessed, but part of me knows I have backed out of the whole mystery of the creation of life. In that sense, our way of life isn't very commendable, is it. Having sex without children. I'm sick to death now of seeing pregnancy as an atom bomb, or the sword of Damocles hanging over you. I'd love to be able to afford the luxury of getting romantic, or of just letting it happen.

GEORGINA I was twenty-five when it happened to me. I never thought it would happen to someone who's so sensible. And I was so moral and puritanical about it too, with other people. It was a long time since my first love, Dave. I'd gone off the Pill after about three years because of what happened to you, Carol. I rather went to pieces, though, using the cap. But I had never really pushed it much, till I met Robert. That was one of those pow, wham, bang, very sexual things, great fun and there I was thrown into a new, very big relationship. We decided to get a flat together. I remember one day, walking down the road with him, sneaking a sideways glance and thinking, 'Here I am with a long-haired guy in blue jeans, who wants to travel and have fun, and wants a girl to do it with. Why not stay with him?' I did stay with him.

We arranged to go away together that summer for the Big Travel. Only a few weeks, but even so a big adventure. We always had a healthy sex life and I remember it was a drag having to take the cap and creams with me in a rucksack. I worried about how I would be able to keep it clean, and how I'd manage to have enough cream with me. The cap was also a bore because he and I used to get thrush together, which had to be a reaction either to the rubber or the cream. But I wasn't going back on the Pill and Copper 7s weren't around then. I'd already worked out we didn't need to use the cap before or after a period. We'd refined its use to fit ours.

While we were away I felt very relaxed. We were mixing with all sorts of hippy, on-the-road people. I didn't do anything wrong but, when we were a week from returning, and staying in a city, I knew my period was due so I forgot the cap. The days passed, and passed, and no period came. I just gave up using the cap altogether. For ages I thought I must have got pregnant then. But in the end I realized it must have been one day, a couple of weeks before, when we were sleeping out in sleeping bags, and he tried to get into mine, but only half made it. We had a half screw, as I called it. As far as I was concerned he never came inside me. Something got in though. A couple of days later I had a faint turn which must have been the moment of conception.

I did not think I was pregnant. We got back home and I was annoyed I hadn't come on as my stomach was fat from being blown up ready for a period. My breasts and stomach always blow up, so there was no difference. It was a difficult time because we were looking for a flat together in London. I just let the time drift by. I can't believe it now. I'd missed periods as a teenager through emotional distresses and I put it down to that. After my second missed period, I went to my GP who prescribed a tonic, or iron tablets, saying I was probably run down! He said to come back a week later if I still hadn't come on. That weekend, you came to London, Heather, and you took one look at me when I said I had to leave a café we were in because I felt faint, and said, 'Are you pregnant?' I nearly wept on your shoulder because I could admit it to myself then. I just hadn't dared admit it. That kind of thing didn't happen to me.

I went to the local hospital to get a test done, and had my first moment of horror. The ante-natal clinic was full of women with fat stomachs and wailing children, waiting for hours. I just thought, 'Oh no, I don't want to be like one of them, like cows all waiting to be milked.' Yet, when I phoned back, and was told it was positive, I was thrilled. You see, for a girl like me, it was like passing an exam really well. I was already so far removed from what 'normal' women were like that to be proven fertile was a real affirmation of womanhood. I'd never thought I'd be able to get pregnant, simply because I'd been having sex for five or six years and had never been pregnant. I said then that over-education leads to complete ignorance of it all.

I had my positive test. My intellectual morality said that if I got pregnant I'd never have an abortion because one must take responsibility for one's actions. I had the impending move to the flat, and a still fairly unknown man, and I had a new job. I told Robert. We had a very romantic walk in some fields when he said he was really quite pleased, and he kissed my stomach, and said he wanted us to get married. Oh dear, I could weep for his sake now. Because I remember feeling, 'But I don't want to get married, and I don't want to lose that job, and I don't want to be stuck with a screaming baby in some grotty bedsit in London.' I still felt too young to get tied down like that.

He went back to his place and the next day it rained. I was no longer in the romantic green meadows. I reached for the phone, to get you, Polly. I knew that I only had to plug into our own underground and help would be there. You came round and said

'You don't want all those yucky milk bottles and all that stuff you have to have like nappies, and prams, and baby walkers, do you?' You were shocked I even thought of having the baby. I honestly don't know what I feel about it now. Then, it was quick. I was already twelve weeks gone. If there is one number girls of our age know, it's the magical thirteen weeks when it's too late. I had to move fast, and somehow that sense of urgency made it all the more important to do so. I don't even know whether I maybe felt I had to have an abortion because it was an experience I should have. I even felt if I walked round with a pregnant stomach other women would look at me crossly and think 'Why didn't she have an abortion?' It seemed more positive to abort than to let this mistimed pregnancy take over my life, stop me doing things. But I'm not sure if it wasn't really all motivated by the excitement of seeing if I could get one fixed up.

Once decided, I was definite. I told Robert and he accepted it with some relief. My lady GP turned tail on me. She was appalled when I said I wanted an abortion. I was twenty-five and if I ever wanted a family I should do so now because, if I left it any later, my children would be teenagers when I was having the menopause – which seemed a roundabout logic. And wasn't I aware it was illegal? There was not a national health doctor who would touch me. I'd have to go to one of the private clinics. I left that place in tears.

What struck me was that she'd advised me to come off the Pill because of my health, and now she was leaving me to go my own way. I could have used a backstreet abortionist for all she knew. I was frightened of the private clinics. It all seemed so sordid. I really didn't see why this one particular episode of my life should be sordid when others hadn't been. I didn't feel guilty or wrong. My plans did not include being a mother at this stage. I wanted to get on with my career.

In the end, through a friend of Heather's, I was put in touch with a good gynaecologist. I went to him privately and there the whole picture changed. He was nice, charming, urbane, gave me a short 'naughty girl' lecture, examined me properly and treated me as a human being. He completely surprised me by saying, in view of my medical history, he would get me a national health one. I was in hospital within three days. Having rushed round town to sign the lease on a flat, gone to two parties and stayed up all night, I walked straight into the hospital and fell asleep. I got a single room. The nurses treated me fine. The operation was neat, clean, simple, unfussy. I was shaved and enemaed, put into a white nightie, and the next thing I knew I was coming round with a drip attached and a feeling of euphoria. I'd been feeling very sick for the past two weeks, and it was magic. The sick feeling had instantly gone. All I felt then was complete relaxation and utter, utter relief. That problem was over. Robert came to visit that night and sat holding my hand looking very worried. It was the drip made me look bad. All my friends came to visit me. I stayed in for over a week. I just felt good to be treated so well, and full of praise for NHS abortions.

I realized then that half the guilt girls feel is because they are told to feel it. At no point, up to thirteen weeks, did I think I was going to have a *baby*. I felt sick, which was a nuisance. But I didn't feel the live growing thing, so I didn't associate the two. Already, only a couple of years after the Act, I felt it was my right. After a week, when my breasts filled up, I woke up one morning crying and crying. I'd had a dream that I'd lost Robert. It was a feeling of pure loss I was experiencing as the hormones readjusted themselves. I went back home, having told neither my parents nor the people I worked with. I changed to my new job, moved in with Robert, felt frightened by all these changes – and just so, so relieved I wasn't having a baby as well, there and then. 'One day', I told myself, 'one day – I'm too young yet.'

7 Drug days

From beatnik, to dolly, to hippy. The days of the mini-skirt were over by 1967. All that flash, brash, groovy life seemed empty and shallow. It was not free, nor liberated in the wider sense. We were entering another world now in which boys and girls walked together – partners against the common enemy, Them.

It had started around the time of Bob Dylan, and picked up pace because of Vietnam. Soon, our lives were taken over with preoccupations of politics and alternative life-styles. Not that any of our group was exactly political. But we talked about politics, along with everyone else. We no longer wanted to be seen as empty-headed, flirtatious people who showed their knickers. We did not want boys who saw us that way either. We began to tone down our image, taking to long, floppy skirts, growing our hair long and natural, trying to look gentle, peaceful and hip in the new way.

We were merging towards the men, and they towards us – meeting half way. The new male hero was no longer the he-male, but the gentle, loving freak. The man who won a woman's heart had long hair and those passive doe-like eyes of the dope head. He was not going to come on masculine with you, but come to you as an equal. He expected a girl to have been around, done her own thing, have her own ideas.

One thing we wanted in our early twenties was adventure. The place to get adventure in 1967 and '68 was America, or at least abroad and not Britain. Flower power had hit America but in English provincial towns such a romantic notion never really came to life. We read about it, listened to their music, but in our lives it was the late 60s movement towards student politics that took priority.

HEATHER When I was with Benny, I used to smoke a lot of dope. Having grown up in the fairground world he'd had quite a conservative upbringing really and a very sheltered life. He'd never met a woman who smoked before. He wanted to try it but needed someone who could show him. He used to buy a hell of a lot though. We used to stay up till three every night. I realized how good it made sex with him! The trouble was I had to get up at 7.30 a.m. to go to work. I was assistant head of the sociology department at school at the time.

I had my first drugs experience at seventeen with Powerful Pierre in Folkestone. I think at that age the idea of taking drugs was so alien that the natural thing was to say I didn't because of my straight background. Obviously, drugs were a status symbol to me. I went out with that heroin addict back at home who used to fix. He showed me the track marks. I didn't really have anything to do with drugs till my third year at university.

The first real drop-out I went out with was Don, who actually latched on to me. He was part of the Liverpool 8 scene – all those poets living on social security. We used to go back to people's flats, to their pads, where it was all to do with rock music and smoking. I didn't know what to do. I didn't know how to go 'phew, phew, phew' – you know, inhaling deeply and noisily. If anyone had asked me to roll a joint I couldn't have done. Except I was curious and started smoking in the end. I was twenty by then though – quite old.

Don walked into my life, put his arm round me and said, 'I'm going to protect you.' I needed it. That is the drugs world, of course. It's cosy and womb-like. You sit around in this beautiful creamy haze. You're insulated. In it everything becomes really smooth. It turned me on to smoking. It wasn't like drinking because it was to do with a heightened sensuality, but I must admit I was totally dependent on men for it. You couldn't go out and score it for yourself. And I never learned to roll a joint properly.

POLLY We've never gone out to score, have we?

HEATHER No. To me it's a bit like the last vestige of chivalry. It's them walking on the outside of the pavement. And you let them because it's illegal and you don't want to get busted! I never actually felt part of the drugs scene. It was its own world with its own language. I indulged myself in it but, because the majority of people I knew didn't smoke, I was different. Going off and doing something dangerous. I didn't smoke again till I got involved in a late-night parties scene just after university, where it seemed the ultimate aim was to become senseless. About ten people – this was the real student life, wasn't it – would meet in a flat and put on very loud progressive rock music. Emerson Lake and Palmer, Pink Floyd, Quintessence. Everybody would end up against the wall, absolutely paralytic. I can remember being so stoned that I had to concentrate all my energies to get to the loo. And the drugs squad coming round to your flat and finding Georgina's packet of Pills in the dustbin.

I'm attracted to men who smoke, I suppose because they are sophisticated. It does have its appeal. I felt then I was acquiring a certain worldliness and I enjoyed it. The crowd I was going round with were graduates in the psychology department and they were experimenting with mescalin as a way of uncovering people's hang-ups. It was so funny. One Sunday morning, we were all handed these little tabs. I looked at mine, thinking all I have to do is take this and something weird is going to happen to me, something totally out of my control. Then I realized I'd taken it and not seen anyone take theirs. After twenty minutes everything went very funny. We went out for a walk and what it did was colour my sense of reality.

I imagined that tripping would be like walking in a very vivid dream world. It was, except you were aware you were tripping. The way it affected me was it gave time this elasticity, so moments of time became not then and the future. It went backwards and forwards. You can see it when you're walking along. I can remember thinking 'It's all just a sensory aberration. Nothing is really happening to my head, it's just things feel and look different, so I perceive them differently.' All of a sudden, people stand out as stereotypes of themselves, which is why you have to be careful who you're with. You can see through them. See the skeleton of their particular characteristics.

I can remember resolving the world's problems. It had an effect on my perceptions of space and time. I think it's our difficulty in grasping them that keeps us from really understanding existence. Anyway I sussed it all out and I opened my mouth to tell somebody, but all those little ideas popped like soap bubbles. I came back and wrote that letter to Georgina. The real message was, 'Dear Georgina, I'm writing to you because I said I would.' It was the ultimate because it was about 'being'. So much of our lives is living out pasts or futures, not being in the present. I also wrote, 'I'm watching the cat being asleep.' When you take a drug it heightens whatever mood you're in. It doesn't take you out of yourself. Then, it was the time that all the anti-acid stuff came out in the press. About how it would give you deformed children. I spent a long time working out that having your own children was an ego trip, and that if I wanted them I could adopt. But I also decided not to take acid again.

POLLY Drugs certainly is a male thing. Like the drinking in a way. And rock music too. It's all part of that aggressive male thing. Part of you thinks 'fuck off' and part of you thinks 'yes, I want it'. I always put down my whole trouble with drugs to my nausea phobia. I hated myself for that because part of me wanted to be groovy and yet I was saying to myself 'I don't *like* this.' I was jealous and my reaction was to do the typical little woman bit. The men would be sitting around getting stoned and there would be me, stone cold sober, thinking 'You inconsiderate pigs!'

I tried to smoke a bit of dope with Mick, but I was heavily into Valium. That sounds like a real druggy! But it was only a neurotic's dependence. It was only with Jeff, who smoked every day and never ever drank that I began to smoke a little. I got stoned with Jeff. He 'turned me on' as the phrase goes. It wasn't long-lasting though. As soon as the relationship broke up, my fears of dope came back. The relationship had been so awful and I felt inadequate all the way through. That was partly because I couldn't get stoned and be laid back too! I reacted against him and felt angry. A terrific conflict in me. The part of me saying, 'Come on, you've got to be cool about this.' And all the time I was thinking, 'What sort of state is he in when he's stoned the whole time?'

After a while with Jeff, I got into this other thing. By then it was 1972 and you could actually say 'it's groovy *not* to smoke'! Particularly if you could be identified with the macrobiotic yoga freaks, who didn't smoke because they didn't want to pollute their bodies. So I tried to convince myself I was part of that trip. Which I wasn't either, really. I would be cooking the brown rice, with Jeff's Indian scarf wrapped round my head, and I could pretend 'I don't need drugs, man!' (*Howls of laughter*)

Anyway, one night we went to a concert at the Rainbow – to see Mountain. We went with a bunch of freaks who were on the dole, you know, making cushions. They had a sporadic income, and seemed unafraid of making money on the side. I was very impressed by them. I mean I was still working in publishing, earning quite a lot, and I couldn't manage on my money. I was always overdrawn and frittered money away on the part of me that got off on taxis, and *Vogue*, and Benson & Hedges – instead of rollies. The whole glamour trip. I had this terrible battle going on between the two sides. I wasn't wholly me with Jeff, nor wholly me with publishing.

I took some speed to go to that concert though. That was the best night on drugs I ever had. Jeff and I were very much together and happy that night so it was all right. He was a real old hand at drugs and even hinted he would take H if he could. I was very envious of his whole hippy thing. I kept thinking, 'What is an experience like that *like*?' I would love to dare to do something like take acid. But I can't and won't. I took that speed partly because I felt confident enough and partly because I thought 'Come on, Polly, let's get a bit out of my head.'

By the time I left the concert I could hardly stand up. We went back to a friend's flat and he was smoking tincture. You know, burning it, that whole alchemical number. I had that feeling I quite often get, 'If only my father could see me now!' All the middle class in me was coming out thinking 'Ha, ha, ha, I'm with the druggies! I'm hitting the underground big time.' I wasn't at all, of course. That morning Jeff and I nearly got picked up by the police. He was loaded and I remember also thinking, 'Ugh, this is illegal. I could actually go to jail for this.' It didn't really worry me because all the responsibility was his. I didn't have dope on *me*, ever.

I've met quite a few women who are into drugs since then, particularly in the travelling theatre crowd. Not only into drugs, but dealing in a big way. But the only time I've been into drugs is with men. If there isn't a man around I tend not to smoke. I don't consciously seek men who smoke but I hardly know any who don't. Dope is sophistication and coolness in a man to us, isn't it?

GEORGINA I would love to know whether we girls got involved in drugs, politics, Flower Power, the new rock music – any or all of it – because we felt the urge to do so, or because men were getting involved and we had to follow? Did we choose to be interested in that kind of man because he was in the kind of world we wanted to be in? Or did we start any of the changes? I know I'd begun by then to go for something more feminine in the man. There was a definite moment when I thought 'I'm fed up with the sods, the macho-types. What I want is one of those gentle, long-haired, doe-eyed, doped-up, cool guys you see hanging around.' It was uni-sex, wasn't it? We fancied the androgynous in each other. We were similar kinds of people. We'd done the same things. We didn't want polarized 'him Tarzan, me Jane' stuff.

In Manchester, in 1968, we had demos about everything. Student grants, the keeping of secret files, race, Vietnam. We had sit-ins which were great fun. It was exciting. It gave us a role in the world. Busloads went down to Grosvenor Square – though not me, I was too lazy. I don't think I ever actually went to a demo. I'm not the involved type. It was status to be political then, though. My parents told a friend's mother that I was becoming lefty and they were rather worried. But I had only picked up the jargon and used to mouth it loudly at home. I was prickly with my parents about everything and we were growing apart. It was genuinely hard to be with people who could not get angry about Vietnam, who would watch TV programmes about South Africa without kicking the set in about apartheid. I had a West Indian boyfriend at the time. Not deliberately, I'm sure. But I told them about him because I was proud of myself. I'd outgrown their image of me as the nice daughter, the educated, well-mannered girl who some day would still make some nice man a nice wife. I started to get scruffier. Baggy jeans and loose, sloppy T-shirts with no bra underneath. Straggly hair. Long skirts that swept the ground. Dun colours. Those Biba colours. I knew I was rebelling against looking 'pretty' or the kind of girl a man 'dates'. The one thing I did not want to look in those days was – dread word – 'bourgeois'. To look bourgeois was the biggest sin!

In the days I still wore make-up, I remember one very poignant scene. It was Christmas Day. I was hurrying to open my father's present. The paper fell off something gilt and shiny. I looked down to see a powder compact, of the type my mother uses. One of those things made of gold, or silver, tucked in a felt purse. Inside was a cake of pink face powder with the little powder puff and a mirror to look at your nose in. I was never going to use one of those objects again in my life. It stood for a type of frivolous femininity that I could hold no truck with. I wasn't too boyish or ballsy, I hope, but I wasn't that type of woman either. I felt very sad to know that my father still hoped I would develop into one of those dainty, glamorous, feminine ladies whose laughter would tinkle graciously, whose demeanour would be alluring, tempting, docile and essentially decorative.

A year later, I gave up make-up altogether. I had been on holiday to Greece and realized I had not thought about using even mascara for eight weeks. When I got home and looked in the little plastic make-up bag I had carried round with me and saw the mess the eyeliners, mascaras, eye shadows, blush-ons and pan-stick had made, all glued together, molten, and sticky I uttered my last 'ugh'. I had never been able to put it on properly. It was like giving up sugar. For a few weeks people asked if I was ill, because my eyes looked weak. Now, I never even think about it. I walk past cosmetic counters in department stores and feel a race apart from those other women. I consider it one of my greatest personal liberations.

POLLY Remember Kev, my beatnik? Well, it was because of him I first got into wearing jeans and floppy sweaters. The beatniks were the hippies or freaks of today. I remember my sister saying when I was eighteen or nineteen, 'When you get to twenty-five you'll smarten up.' And I said, 'Oh no, I shall always be a scruffy freak!' I did smarten up for a while when I went to work in publishing. I was twenty-two and into the professional world. I definitely went through a phase of wanting to be trendy, groovy, and to have the most fashionable clothes. All through my early twenties, I wanted to marry Mick, get a flat or a house in Hampstead, have Habitat furniture and Biba clothes. It was that sort of image. It was the young London number. The swinging 60s rather than the hippy 60s. I went into publishing as a compromise. I really wanted to be an actress but I got this job and it meant status and financial security. It was less demanding work. It was just an exciting job for me. I remember saying 'I don't know why my father complains about my clothes and appearance because, after all, I could have been a dropped-out freak, smoked dope all the time, and hung around the pop festivals with beads round my neck.'

I dabbled with the Flower Power thing a bit, in the summer of 1967. It wasn't happening in Manchester. The nearest I got to it was in Brighton. There were flowers-in-their-hair hippies there. I put on my jeans, with my black satin shirt, long silk scarves, and every string of beads I could find. With my hair loose, I walked through Brighton. I hadn't the confidence to wear those clothes anywhere else. Until then I'd been ironing my hair and sellotaping it down laboriously to get the swinging, trendy look. The hippy thing brought in curly hair. Great for me, but, even so, it took a long time to get through into the trendy look.

GEORGINA I didn't get involved in the drugs world in any way as a rebellion, for the simple reason I was too scared. I've never taken acid and never would. I took some coke last year with Martin only because I am so much under his sway. Real 'candy man' stuff he is. I trust him and would do anything, I suppose. Actually I loved it. I'd do it again now if I had the money. It made sex fantastic. But I'd never use it a lot.

Drugs was a problem to me because people I admired or wanted to go around with were getting into the whole number – talking a new jargon which I didn't feel I could use until I had at least gone through the initiation rites. 'Turning on' was a phrase used then rather like 'falling in love'. People said it had happened to them. And no-one was ever sure whether they'd achieved what other people had. Still, you learned to bluff. It was part of status and image. Once, at a party of my parents' friends, we young ones, the students, were asked if we'd smoked 'pot'. I actually lied and said I had because I wanted them to think of me in that way. I wanted to be brave enough. But in fact there was not very much around in Manchester in 1968. You had to be very underground to smoke regularly then.

My real initiation came in 1968 in America. Robert Kennedy had been killed in the spring and Washington DC, where I went, had riot police out with guns, shields, and a curfew after 10 p.m. Another illusion of peace and love shattered. It was that summer that Russia invaded Czechoslovakia too. It was the Flower Power time, I remember, because I stayed with a group of artists who staged 'happenings'. On this particular night, the happening took the form of a treasure hunt round the nation's monuments. The organizer had left notes hidden which gave instructions like 'Run round the Lincoln Memorial twenty times in a northerly direction then proceed to . . .' There was a map drawn of the route to be taken. It was great fun, on a hot night in sweaty Washington. Except we did not know about the events taking place in Prague right at that time. The Washington police were on guard for trouble. They found some of the maps and decided it was a plot to blow up the monuments. We were all roped in, caught running round the Lincoln Memorial! The not so gentle looking police gave us a thorough interrogation, fingering their triggers. The organizer's wife kept calling the man with the itchy trigger finger a 'pig' – and all the daffodils, and flowers in our hair, would not have made for peace and love that night.

What I'd gone to see, though, was Haight Ashbury. That summer, and the year before, had been all California Dreamin' and Sergeant Pepper. California was meant to have the answer. I hitch-hiked across the States with another English girl I met out there. I'd hitch-hiked before of course. Never on my own, I'm not that brave really. But you get used to the various dangers involved. I usually go into those situations with an air of calculated naiveté. If you expect the best of people, you tend to get the best in return. It was the approach we learned from the old days going round with rockers and teds. They could have been violent or dangerous but, as we assumed they were nice, sensitive human beings, they usually were to us.

Hitching in the States was more exciting and more dangerous than anywhere else. Everyone knew the stories about the dreadful things that could happen. At the same time, it seemed ridiculous to be stopped from travelling that way because of some imagined danger. Hitching is fun, it's cheap, and it's the best way to get to know a country because you go with the people who live there. If you go by bus or train you're anaesthetized from the country and its people. You've bought yourself right of passage, and limited yourself to your own company and perceptions. As it happened, Doreen and I had an Adventure in America, with a capital 'A'.

We travelled south, through the Carolinas and Georgia, across the middle of the prairie lands into the cowboy country, ending up one day in a dive bar near Laramie, doing the Jitterbug with real cowboys. We went to Texas next and I got scared there. I insisted we took a bus at one point across the wasteland where we couldn't even see any towns marked on the map. Then, from El Paso, we hitched a ride that we knew, by all the rules of the road, we should not have taken.

It was night, and you never take rides at night. It was a truck, and, unlike British lorry drivers, American truck drivers are not gentlemen of the road. He was a lone, freelance truck driver and, at most, hitchers' rules in the States are that any truck should belong to a company because the drivers have to check in and out with their bosses along the road. Rides in America last for thousands of miles, so anything can happen. Doreen and I got in with him though. We climbed in the high front seat of his cab and set off into the blackness of the night. Doreen went to sleep in the compartment at the back of the cab. I rode up-front with him, chatting all the way about life back home, putting over what a nice girl I was, talking about my boyfriend. You have to have a boyfriend when you're hitching. He thought we were runaways or girls of the road so I did my best to dispel those ideas. In fact, my blond haired truck driver was quite reasonable. He talked to me about New Mexico, pointed out the rattle snakes and the Indian reservations and asked me if I wanted to take some speed. I was horrified at the idea and said no, though the last thing I wanted to do was go to sleep. But, of course, as we drove along, off the main route then, I became sleepy and my eyes blurred over. I came to convinced the truck was still moving and I was in the cab on my own.

I was just sliding into the driver's seat to take control of the empty vehicle, when he opened the door on my side and asked if I'd get out to hold his torch while he checked his brakes. 'May as well help,' I thought. Standing outside in the arid scrub desert of New Mexico, the thought flashed through my mind like a newsreel, 'What are you doing here?' We were off the main road. If he murdered us we might not have been found for weeks, or years. No-one knew I was hitch-hiking. My parents would be so upset, not only at my death, but at the fact I'd brought it on so tragically and so early by my obstinate stupidity. We would lie there with vultures pecking at our eyes. When they found our bodies we'd be unrecognizable. Unknowns.

Still, I was completely surprised when he suddenly took hold of my shoulders and pinned them against the side of the truck. 'Georgina,' he said, 'do you want to make love?' It's funny what you actually think about in moments of real crisis. I'd dreamed about such things many times, and fantasized my escape route. But you never know what it will feel like until it actually happens. For a start, you never expect to be asked such a question. I instinctively wanted to giggle. I was so inexperienced no man had ever asked me that, even at a party. So I said 'No.' Then his grip tightened. I began to fret a bit.

Tears came into my eyes, as I realized that not only would we be murdered but raped too. Just as the tears were welling up, luckily my senses came back to me. I told myself if there was a time for keeping a cool head this was it. It might be a question of life or death. For one thing, I worked out, he was big and strong. So I could not fight my way out. I could not snivel and cry my way out either. Nor could I turn aggressive as that might lead him on. I did wonder how he meant to do anything with me out there in the desert with the rattlesnakes around. But, even so, I knew I'd rather give in to him and say yes than be raped. I wasn't a virgin, I'd had one or two lovers since Dave. I was on the Pill. No real danger. It might not be so awful.

In that same flash second, I had an idea. I snivelled again and when he said 'Why not?' I came back with the answer 'Because I'm a virgin.' At once his arms relaxed and he let me go. He asked me if I thought Doreen might. And, as I felt she'd got me into this, I said yes. She was braver than me anyway. We walked back to the cab and I found her sitting at the driver's wheel. She was working out how *she* could drive the truck off after I'd been murdered! He asked her the same question and in her funny northern accent she shrieked 'Who do you think you are?' So he drove on. When we saw the next truck stop, we asked to pull in to go to the toilet. As he opened the door, we took our bags to get down and run for it. He said quietly, 'You're not going, are you?' I felt sorry for him. He was lonely. Maybe we'd over-reacted. All he'd done was ask.

We got to Los Angeles and San Francisco unscathed, with more ridiculous adventures along the way. But San Fransisco was where we wanted to be.

HEATHER I know what you mean about hitch-hiking. I go out on my own a lot and I know I'll be all right because I switch on the survivalist vibes.

GEORGINA Why do you hitch on your own, though? It is more dangerous, isn't it?

HEATHER It's necessity. You don't think so? OK. It's something you do once and once done is easy. I enjoy hitching on my own. I enjoy going through life on my own. You meet people. It's a challenge. You're with a guy in a car and if you play it one way you're OK. Another way and you lose. One of the last times I hitched up to Wales for the weekend, I nearly had a bad time. I got lots of little lifts. One middle-aged man got very red in the face and offered me money to do things with him. I stayed very cool and said unfortunately he'd asked the wrong person. I thought 'If I act shocked I'm inviting his guilt to direct itself sadistically on to me.' So I tried to be cool. That was a close shave because he was a bit nutty. Apart from that it's just randy people, and the moment you mention their wife and kids, you create a different situation.

People say girls who hitch are courting danger. You can play it to minimize or maximize the danger. I never say where I'm going till they've said. For me, it's usually so I can get from A to B as cheaply as possible. But on the other hand, I suppose I wouldn't go to those places till I'd saved the bus fare if I were really concerned. It's sad that yet again we can't just admit that we like the danger, but men can. If we say we want danger, it tends to sound as if we want sex really.

The nearest I ever came to being raped was when I went to look for a flat once. Polly's Mick was with me, I think. He was outside in the pub. This landlord character took me in and was showing me a revolting flat. He offered me a sherry and I thought 'May as well be nice to the poor guy.' He sat on the bed and suddenly he grabbed hold of my hand and was saying how nice I was. It takes a moment before you register what's going on. A moment too late – he had me on that bed and was holding me under him. I remember struggling. He was obviously going to rape me. He was saying revolting things like 'Girls like you really want it, so why fight it?' They always use that line. What I did realize was that in cases of rape they've got gravity on their side. If you're under and they're bigger than you, it's hard to fight when you're on your back. I'd have fought all the way. What I did do was use my head. I talked him out of it quite calmly saying I'd scream and my friend was outside, and how it would ruin him as a landlord and I'd get the police. I wasn't aggressive. Just middle class and sensible. Actually, all that happened was, just as I was about to give in, he looked at his watch and said

'Oh, I've got to go out.' I staggered out to Mick, who was asleep in the car, and told him what had happened. When he heard how big the bloke was, he decided to take me for a brandy! Rape seems to be inevitable to me. I was just lucky.

GEORGINA I had another near rape, now you mention it. When I was going round with black guys. It was not pre-meditated. But you go with one West Indian and you tend to get involved with others. I went for two years once without seeing white flesh in bed by me. I got quite frightened I'd never fancy white skin again. It seems ugly after some lovely brown skin. Anyway, this guy was African and very competitive. If the others had been out with me I think he felt he ought to be able to say he had too. He was the big wheeler and dealer and semi-crook. Something about his evilness attracted me. It was scoring points on the experience stakes. It was a dreadful evening. He'd borrowed someone's car to drive me to a restaurant out of town. The car's headlamps didn't work properly. He kept staring at me with this awful glint in his eyes. I couldn't get away though as we were miles from anywhere. I should have run for my life. I remember the drive home and I was thinking 'Please God, just let me get home and I'll be a good girl from now on, marry some bank clerk or something. Just don't let me die now, tonight. It would be such a waste.' Well, we got back to town but I wasn't home yet. He drove back to his place. I said 'But it's late and I want to go straight home.' He wouldn't take me, I had to come in for coffee first. I mean I knew it was a ruse but I still trusted his better nature. So I went in. He grabbed me into this chair he was sitting in. But I wouldn't even kiss him because I hated him so much by then. He kept fondling me, trying to soften me up. I just kept up my nice girl thing. I mean I'd only had the one West Indian boy-friend, who was a really sweet guy, so he didn't have any reason to think I'd go with anyone. In the end, to my surprise, he gave in and drove me home. I haven't been in a spot like that since. That's one reason a girl buys her own car. You know that way you can get home!

POLLY Just recently, I've gone more rebellious and have been with weirder men. Not so long ago, I had a brief thing with a really freaked out black drummer who sat drumming for hours, giving me these side glances, until he'd worked himself, and me, up into a frenzy. But I don't like the aggressive male thing. I just tend to be thinking when I'm with a man like that 'I wonder what Daddy would say if I took *him* home!' My last man was like that. We met and within a day were in love. Zed, my mystical freak, in his yellow bus, which was lined with brown velvet and smelled heavily of incense. He was more into dope than anyone I'd ever seen. I couldn't even place where he came from. He was the real traveller. Very pale, with black kohl on his eyes, and his hair was hennaed. Only when he grew a beard did he look like the blond German he was. I couldn't really get into the freak world, though. I'm too straight. Zed had kicked it all, and that's why he's hopeless to relate to.

GEORGINA Like me with Haight Ashbury. Of course it was a shock and a disappointment. This was not the beautiful scene I'd expected. There were no flowers, or peace, or love. The streets were tatty, the people looked dead. Too many wasted addicts hanging around. Kids with their eyes glazed over and their faces old. Doreen and I joined in the life a bit. We went to the local hospital to give blood because we could earn eight pounds a pint for our best blue English blood. The waiting room was full of addicts who were turned back because of hepatitis, or because they'd given blood in the last three months. They looked filthy and sad.

The hospital itself was even more alarming, as we saw sights there no English person really knew about then. Dressed in the blue uniform of inmates, we saw young men with no legs, with no arms, with faces blown to pieces. Suddenly the reason why they needed our blood was obvious. America was fighting a real war, over the ocean. Vietnam was not just TV news. Young men were dying or being maimed for it. We felt sick inside. We'd heard of draft dodgers but this was all so different from anti-Vietnam demos.

We met a couple of guys and went back to their Haight Ashbury pad. I remember going through one of those hippy-style rainbow painted doors that had slogans about drugs scrawled over it, up grimy stairs, to a grubby sort of room with mattresses on the floor. I wasn't bothered by that. The guys I knew in Manchester were all living in grubby rooms where you could sit back and listen to early blues music. I think I smoked my first joint then. I doubt if I even got stoned. I was too scared to inhale!

One lasting memory of that scene was listening to a record. I thought it was a black woman singer and I loved the Supremes, and Dionne Warwick and Loraine Ellison then. But it was Janis Joplin, white, gutsy and only just on the scene. *Cheap Thrills* had just come out. When I got back, the first thing I did was buy it. Janis Joplin came to mean a lot to me.

Janis knew exactly what it meant to be a gutsy, ballsy girl, to want to do everything the boys did, and then to suffer because she was not feminine enough. She knew all about those pent-up feelings that you can only get out in the big scream, about the claustrophobia that comes from a straight upbringing and background. When, after she died, Myra Friedman wrote the book about her, I loved its title – *Buried Alive*. 'Kozmic Blues' is my all-time favourite:

Time keeps movin' on
Friends, they turn away
I keep movin' on, but I never found out why
I keep pushin' so hard an' babe, I keep tryin'
To make it right to another lonely day.

. . . They ain't never gonna love you any better, babe
And they're nee-ever gonna love you ri-ight
So you better dig it right now, right now. Oohhh.

Janis never found relationships with men easy. She was a plain girl who wanted to be loved as a girl, who wanted deep down to be thought of as pretty. No man, she would say, could ever give her what she sang about – 'Fill me like the mountains, fill me like the sea . . .' – the rush, the filling, the geyser of love, that she got from the audience and the audience from her. The cosmic moment to send away the Kozmic Blues. Janis once said, 'Housewives in Nebraska have pain and joy; they've got soul if they give into it. It's hard. And it isn't a ball when you do.' I loved her.

You do find those cosmic moments sometimes, though, if you wait. I found it with Martin recently.

POLLY That's what happened with Zed. He and I immediately had this romantic trip that we'd run away together. It was my ultimate expression of freedom. But what happened? Three weeks together in some isolated cottage and we were fighting like cats and dogs, hurling abuse, insults and weapons at each other. I got frightened I wouldn't be able to escape. It is very, very hard to know what it is you want, isn't it.

8 Life among the men

GEORGINA The first job I ever had was in a shop but I soon moved to being a waitress in a café because it was more fun. You had more autonomy. We were schoolgirls, being paid three shillings an hour. I've never had quite so much fun since. We just didn't care. The main concern was to get as many laughs out of the day as possible. We used to pin paper serviettes to our heads, mimicking the waitress style, then go through the large café room doing the Conga. We cooked up disgusting concoctions in the milk shake mixer and served them out to see what customer reaction was. We aimed all our powers of charm and persuasion on one table to see if the poor man would leave us a tip. We gave free meals to our boyfriends, and must have been incredibly hard to handle, slipping out of the net like eels once we were caught, especially if it was the shop manager, who was always trying to chat us up. 'Poor greasy fellow,' we called him. By the time I was in my next job, in a big department store, serving on the vegetable counter, I did wonder why the girls got eight pounds a week, when the young guys got twelve pounds? Worse was the fact the married women got less than we girl students as ours was tax free. It's funny looking back and thinking of working for unequal pay without a quibble.

POLLY When I was a little girl I wanted to be a café lady. I thought they were the ultimate. We never went in cafés because we couldn't afford them, of course. There was my Aunt Hattie, too, my father's younger sister, who seemed to me to be like a café lady. But although I had a phase of wanting to be a dancer and a nurse, I think I always assumed I'd be a teacher. I mean what else did you do? If you worked hard, passed your exams and went to university, you became a teacher. It was good for women because you could go back after having kids. My mother and grandmother brought me up to think in terms of having a career. They were clever women, not intellectual, but they knew you couldn't really rely on a husband to support you. It was assumed I'd marry, have children, and go back to my teaching. Definitely all still in the woman's role.

GEORGINA My mother was a clever woman. She could have been an academic if she'd carried on. Both her parents died young and she had to go to work in an office, though. She did really well in School Certificates. One of my earliest memories is of her telling me she wanted to become a journalist, but she hadn't been able to. I must have picked it up from her. She'd instilled in me that she read a lot as a young girl, so I felt I ought to, too. I think she wanted me to fulfil the bits she hadn't. She was always an organized woman – on lots of committees and things. I think from early on I realized she could just as easily have put that energy into a male type of job. Still, I didn't have grandiose ideas for myself. I didn't even consider university. We weren't that kind of family.

I do wonder if my mother didn't steer me away from being a housewife and mother into a career woman, though. There was one thing she said when I was a teenager which I remember. We had inherited some furniture and she said to me 'We won't throw it away as one day you'll have a flat of your own and might need it.' My reaction was to nod. But inside I was really angry and thought 'Oh no I won't.'

HEATHER My parents never encouraged me to have a career. My sister wanted to go to university – but that was when it was seen as a complete indulgence for a woman to go to university because women's careers weren't considered important. She took a secretarial course and ended up secretary to an industrial managing director, which she found totally stultifying. I was the only one in the family who went to university. I was the cleverest one.

GEORGINA As a graduate I went for a job in TV where there was no problem of equality. They were recruiting women trainees by then. The first token women in the vanguard of the new consciousness – and, as it was a profession, of course we got equal pay. In TV some girls began as PAs and then worked their way into research jobs from there. But they had to learn to play the game, to be accepted as nice, helpful, hopefully pretty things, please the boss and get on in the world. I remember older women sometimes advised us to start out in our careers in journalism by becoming secretaries, or in TV, as PAs. Crazy. Be warned against it. Once you learn to do somebody else's work, it's a long way back to finding your own self-confidence.

As students we had grown up accepting our equality, hadn't we? Both sexes had very little money so there was no question of being taken out for dinner by a boy, or of letting him buy you drinks. We stood our rounds of drinks and shared the cost of the disgusting curries we ate after the union bar closed. I never wanted to be wooed over dinner in restaurants. I thought it was decadent and bourgeois to be bought in that way. Once, when a man I did not fancy insisted on taking me out for a meal, I said to the girl I shared with 'If he takes me for a curry he's not having it. If it's the Piccadilly I'll have to let him.' We both thought it was very funny, but I was banking on his meanness. He took me for a curry and I couldn't stop laughing all night. I've always wanted to buy my own way in the world, not have some man do it for me.

I've worked in discos and bars before I got into my career because that's the only way to earn good money. But I was never very good as I couldn't master the Smile. The permanent Smile those girls have to keep on. I'm such a stroppy bitch. It was funny recently when Heather asked me how was she going to make a lot of money fast? I said 'Be a Playboy bunny or something,' because she's got the tits. She said sadly, 'Don't you realize we're too *old*! We're thirty. We can never get that sort of job any more.' Jesus, too late already to cash in our femaleness. What a sobering thought.

HEATHER While here I am in that other female role, the poorly paid secretary. It's my choice. I took it to have part-time work so I could paint. But I have to consciously play a part to stop myself going crazy. I'm the secretary-sending-up-the-secretary, and sending up the boss. My boss is a lady killer and so I put him down in a jokey way, and he loves it. He and I have worked out a way of relating where I appear to be taking liberties with him. He hovers round me and I say 'Oh go away, can't you see I'm busy?' and he really loves it. That is totally out of character with the normal boss/secretary thing and with most of his relationships with women. If I ever got involved with him, it wouldn't work of course.

I was very unrealistic when I left university about what I was going to do. I remember I went for interviews in market research and advertising. I'd always thought that teachers were dull middle-class people. Then I got involved and it was intellectually stimulating and meaningful, because it was working with people. I got into teaching by accident when a friend found me a job. But it was a good thing. I had a lot of autonomy. I was assistant head of department at twenty-two. I organized my own working life and it was fascinating. But it was part of the Establishment. I was going out with Benny at the time. One day a young girl I'd had palmed off on me to look after because she had nowhere to live turned the tide for me. I came home and found the bed in a terrible mess and Benny said 'I've got something to tell you.' I thought he'd slept with her. But no, he'd turned her on! I took her aside and said that I'd be grateful if she didn't mention it at work. It was my private life and as far as I was concerned, OK. But it was illegal. Of course she told them this embroidered story about the debauched life I was leading, using every drug under the sun. They actually re-admitted her to hospital to get her away from me. One of the other teachers had been to my head of department and said, 'Do you know Heather's on pot?' She had also said, 'I think that's the least of her problems.' Which was right. I was 'on' Benny. I resigned shortly after that, though.

I was in a career that involved a lot of responsibility and really I was relieved to be out of it. Benny picked me up one night and took me to a hotel to sleep with him. I just thought 'Why not do it? He won't stick around, and it's new experience.' I never expected to see him again, but he came round a few days later. He was a traveller who'd always been in the fairground world. I was first of all interested in him because socially I'd never met a traveller like that. It was he who suggested we went travelling. I chucked in the job as I'm attracted to that way of life, living off your wits. The only thing was, I wasn't a traveller and his family wouldn't accept me. We were going to go round in a caravan. He'd have done his number, and I'd have made and sold things, taught the kids or something. I saw him as somebody who'd give me the opportunity to get involved in a life-style like that. I wasn't in love with him. His pull was that he lifted me out of my boring rut and he was good in bed!

The nice thing about travelling is that you have your own piece of security so you can get up and move on when you want. You don't starve. I loved it most of the time. We used to creep round allotments taking one vegetable from each, and I'd go shoplifting. I'd never have the guts now. We couldn't get work at that time, so we weren't inherently wicked or bad. But if he had a headache, for instance, I used to go to Boots and get aspirin for him! It was like the romantic dream I've always had. It was so healthy. I ate like a horse and lost weight.

Working on the fairgrounds I learned was a real rip-off. We'd stop in a small town and the people would be very friendly towards us. Then they'd play into your hands later on, because you're exotic, something strange and new. They were like rabbits in a trap. Fairground people quite cynically are out to make a fast buck. They make their money by cheating people – short-changing them. You control how fast the music goes, and you take the money just before the machine, say the Whip, starts up and they're only too happy to get their change before they're twizzled off. Benny described it as sickening. As the night went on, the music went faster, the thing went crazier and as he was constantly riding the moving floorboards, he got meaner. You become very conscious in the end that you're making money off those same people who a few hours ago welcomed you so warmly.

But funnily enough, that was one of the most secure times of my life. In the end we ran out of money so I went back to London to get a job for a while. He stayed in the caravan and I used to hitch up to join him. It was a strange experience for me. But when I went back to London once, I bought a copy of *The Times* and saw this job advertised working with young kids who had drug problems. I think I felt like doing something involved in the real world again. I applied, and got it. That was the end of the travelling. I told Benny and he wasn't impressed. He looked at me and said 'You've got me all wrong.' He meant I was getting involved in the Establishment again. I knew at that moment we were different. I had to go my own way.

I was attracted to the whole drugs scene because I wanted to be doing something with a minority group. It was being associated with something trendy. It was a bit like my interest in the occult. Superficial, something to do with wanting to be mysterious and more than my face value. Drugs had a glamour about them at that time. Also I thought *I*'d be able to get through to these people.

I got to know a lot about the drugs world. I saw how it was attractive to people wanting to identify with a close-knit group and wanting to be somebody. When you're doing something illicit and succeeding, you are somebody. So the whole idea of the person who scores is very attractive. That experience in the end, though, made me very cynical and bored with anything to do with drugs. You realize their emotions have become measured in chemical terms. At times I'd find it such a strain that I'd go to my room and think 'Oh give me some barbs!' I think that's why I did drop some acid in the end. In my life I've always had to express the opposites. If I was being a good schoolteacher, then, in my personal life, I had to very irresponsible. I also took some amphetamines once for slimming. But speed frightens me because it is *so* nice. I know I enjoy myself because I am so inconsistent. I enjoy the fact I have relationships with people who would never have the slightest idea I've taken acid!

POLLY I left my first glamorous job in publishing after three years. I wasn't really interested. Somewhere at the back of my mind had always been the artist fantasy, the bohemian life-style, and this wasn't it. I left in 1972. During that time I had been going out with Jeff. He opened the door to me to the hippy world. Although he was a social worker, he was a hippy. He wore Indian smocks, smoked dope, had been to India and ate brown rice. I used to call him a 'walking cliché'. But only because I was jealous.

Suddenly, through him, I got very conscious of my middle-class, trendy, Habitat image. I thought 'I don't want to be like this.' Jeff was saying 'Status is rubbish: self-confidence comes from self-knowledge.' As soon as the seed was planted, I wanted it to grow. I'm about rebellion in many ways. I want everything my father isn't, really. Publishing was full of people who drank themselves silly. Jeff was hard for me in other ways. I couldn't cope with him really. But the hippies were involved in treating their bodies well, were into ecology, and I knew I was going in that direction. I no longer wanted to live in Hampstead: I wanted to live in the country – all that sort of thing.

When I left the job, I went to live with my brother in the country. He and his friends were all into Jungian psychology. It was all Jung, Krishnamurti and Castaneda. Me saying, 'Who am I?' That winter I went into the void, realizing there was a lot more to this than Habitat houses. I wanted an awareness of the unconscious.

I came back to London in 1973 but had the most dreadful time then. I was afraid of the people, the noise, the travelling. I was out of work and didn't know what to do with myself. I read mystical books and dabbled. I'd sleep all afternoon and do anything to fill the day. I wanted to be like those people who live from making the odd cushion. But I couldn't do it. I could hardly live on the dole. I wore blue jeans and a blue polo-necked jumper for nine months! I vaguely thought of going into social work but I was easily defeated when they said 'You've been out of work for six months; are you depressed?' Jeff would come round and I'd say 'I don't know what to do with my life.' And he'd say 'Live it.'

Then I went back into publishing. They rang me up and suddenly I realized I could make some money freelance. It pulled me out of the rut. For the first time, my work there was fairly creative. I could control what I did. I began to share a flat with a girl who is very zappy. I became zappy too. I still had my Biba jeans and T-shirts. But I also had a long scarf and I began to look freaky again. I had a lot of abortive relationships in that period. I tried things like Tai Chi and encounter groups. I was looking for therapy but didn't know it.

I was wanting to find some creative work I could put my energy into. I was much more aware of the world and I could see that the people I worked with were not in touch with themselves. It was all pollution and instant food, and instant books. It connected. There was no heart, no real depth. It still took me nearly two years to make the break. It was at that time I met Don, who Heather had been out with. The poet, who smoked dope all the time. He was a real bohemian, not at all ambitious. With him I managed to say I wasn't into dope and it was OK. It was just one of those things I had to get through with men.

That summer, because of Don, was the year of biggest changes. I met the people from the creative arts group. They played a more important role in my creative change than they know. They had this terrific, almost naïve, enthusiasm. Being creative for them was being spontaneous. They never had the fear that says 'daren't'. Sue does anything and she cracks it. 'Oh you can learn how to do that. It's easy.' That ability to say 'I'll take the chance, so what if we blow it?' I went on tour with them; and it was my first real intro to freak culture. That summer I was in on my last freelance publishing contract. They'd said come to the Bath Festival (actually the Walcot Street Festival in Bath) at the beginning of August. The thing with Don wasn't so good. I was having my fling with the black drummer. It was as if each boyfriend was less and less presentable to Daddy. All part of breaking out.

Bath was my turning point. It was the fact of being on the road, the attraction of the travelling life. That's fifty per cent of the fun. The packing up and going on. It's like childhood camping. You don't wash properly, you live in the open air. We were sleeping where we fell because it was so hot that summer. Often we worked all night, the women making soup for the boys who were putting up the dome. Life with no structure – and it was very attractive. A laid-back life-style. There were no worries. There was a huge kitchen that gave out food whenever you wanted – they were feeding thousands of freaks. The Festival was organized by the Bath Arts Workshop and really it was to do with alternative technology – all the windmills and things. It was there I realized that a lot of people of twenty-eight or nine, intellectual, sensitive people, not hippies, were there with their long hair tied back in pony tails, making domes, living off the land, and making alternative worlds. People our age who were doing something useful. I was being outrageous there – wearing just a bikini with a long scarf round my waist, getting brown, and sweaty, having the odd drag of a joint and being half stoned. It's fun in the fresh air.

I was so excited when I came back from Bath. I was beginning to wear more freaky clothes, but still didn't dare wear them in London. I wore no make-up there. Those rural freak women, with their scrubbed faces and hair in plaits, are not very pretty but they look good because it is such a frank and honest exposure of the self. So, one day, I finally packed up my job at 6 p.m. on a Friday night and caught a train to Penzance to join another travelling arts group. I got there at midnight – into the land of our teenage dreams. I was met by a crowd of gorillas and clowns and musicians. I was taken to a camp by the sea, with the moon shining down on us. For four days I didn't stop to think. I raced about shopping, cooking, wearing clown's clothes, painting faces, loving it all – and I fell in love with Zed. We went together to Watchfield, which was a freaks' festival. Most were the boring type there. It was desolate in a way, but exciting because I'd never been to a freaks' holiday camp before. Thousands of naked people, all very stoned, all very boring if you stayed too long. They do nothing. But the more interesting people are tending to gravitate to the actual Fairs, like Bungay May Horse Fair, a traditional fair revived by latter-day hippies, all New Age crafts and wholemeal foods, side by side with the local people having their horse shows and dog racing. I love them. When I was at Watchfield I did take off all my clothes under the public tap, and I thought 'Who is this person?' But it doesn't mean I can be un-inhibited like that for the rest of my life, or even that I want to.

It was after that, and Zed, that I became very positive and got into my weaving. I knew weaving was *my* thing. It means I have the potential to live off making and selling something – part of the new life movement that has emerged out of the turmoil of the 60s. These people wanted to mate and have children, create homes, but in a new, better and more honest way. Not the way of cars, flats and instant foods. So last summer I got to know those rural commune groups even better. The theatre groups, the country craftsmen. I still don't get out of my head on dope or drink as they do. But I do feel I exist. I'm still playing summer games though. Living out certain fantasies when I'm on the road with them. It's hard to get really involved with them though, unless you've a *man* to do it with!

GEORGINA   It was much more fashionable in the late 60s and early 70s to be anti-career, anti-work altogether. The alternative society had much more appeal after the heady years of '68. I joined the career game feeling very much a traitor as I was the only one who went into it and stayed there!

ME   What about me, too? I became a journalist straight after university with my first job which was on the *Guardian*. It was too much, I remember, my fantasy life coming true. I wanted to be like those women in the 40s movies, who wisecracked with the boss, wore hounds tooth check suits and black velvet hats pinned on the back of their permed hair. I wanted to be Rosalind Russell – straight, hard-talking, tough, pretty. I wanted the life of the quick repartee and jokes that rebounded off me. I got all that – but more too. I also had the incredible day of fantasy before I started work – to think of young Carol from Burton walking down Fleet Street, notebook in hand, smile and charm at the ready. The *Guardian* lot were all northern people too.

But I also remember thinking at that time 'Why me? What am I doing here?' I should have been married by then to some good, kind accountant or bank clerk. Having gone through university as a sort of finishing school – what was the line? 'An educated woman makes a better mother' – and be prepared now to raise some man's children in the world. None of the women in my immediate family had felt the need to push themselves in this way. Why was I forcing myself out of my background?'

GEORGINA   But it felt good to be earning a proper salary. To get monthly pay slips and cheques that were on a par with the men's at my level. That gave me autonomy in my life. I used to spend my money on travelling, mostly, and still do – and clothes. Not on material goodies. I bought one big thing, after a year, a car. That meant my independence was well and truly signed and sealed. But, having that money often made me think how different it was from my mother's housekeeping purse. It was all *my* money, given to me by a boss who could not use it as emotional blackmail. I never had to feel guilty that I was depriving someone else of food or shoes. I'm so used to it now I can't imagine ever changing. I've never taken money from a man. It would seem strange even if it were meant to be for the rearing of *our* child, I know that.

The greatest thing that equal pay gave me was independence. That independence has been a frightening load to handle. I didn't buy a flat, or arrange to find a secure place to live, or save with a building society, for at least six years. I think I know why. It *is* frightening for a woman to be too efficient at setting herself up on her own. It's easier to be vague, to float, to wait for the day a man will come along either to do it with, or to make the arrangements himself. It is hard to be too liberated too early. How can you fit yourself into a man's life or him into yours? Relationships have never been made on those terms in the past. Even my car was bad enough. I was aware as soon as I owned it, that good though a car might be for getting me home from parties, saving me from rape scenes, it also chipped away at whatever bits of dependence were left.

HEATHER Yes, looking back I realize I've been subtly investing in some fantasy man coming along and giving me everything I lacked: like security and stability; material things; somewhere proper to live. I never really seriously considered that I'd ever have to create my own security, that I'd ever have to think about saving for a mortgage or anything like that. For years, in my twenties, I lived in these shared flats or communal set-ups, and it was fine. But I've always had privacy within it, always had a place of my own. I can't imagine now actually setting up with a man. I think the whole 'room of your own' thing did it for me. If I'd never gone away from home to university I'd never have wandered off the beaten track in the way I have. I can remember the kick of first moving into an unfurnished flat and having my own room. Not having anybody else to consider but myself. It's funny to think that's something we took for granted. When I talk to other women who got married, I realize that they've never had that. Never had their own place. In London, they shared rooms with other girls, and then a man moved in and that was that. They've never had any *space*.

POLLY When I first began the whole weaving thing and stopped being well off, I knew poverty was part of the thrill, I had to do it – learn how to live on *nothing*. I'd always been hopeless with money. I didn't have anything to show for it. For the first year of being poor, I really enjoyed it and I began to know other people who were the same. We almost compete to see who's got the cheapest second-hand clothes, the most out of skips, or hitched the furthest. Now, I just accept I'm poor because I can't make any money from what I do, yet. I have to do bum jobs for cash which pisses me off. I do want a bigger flat or to be able to rent a studio.

HEATHER To hear you talk! They're all things you've never mentioned doing before!

POLLY I know. I suppose I'm still hoping a man will come along to do it for me. I'm thirty and learning a new craft. There is a pressure on me to be in a situation now where I can make a home and have a family as well. I don't want to be still like this at thirty-five. So I still do want the 'husband figure'. Maybe he has already got a studio. He'll be prepared in part, as I'm the type of woman who likes cooking, cleaning, and caring for a home, to let me do that in exchange for him bringing some money in from the creative world. I'm old-fashioned in that. I want to have children, so I want to find this husband.

GEORGINA I had the other kind of attitude towards men. I suppose I did put my work first. From the beginning in TV I had to work unsocial hours. I was rather shocked when my boss asked me if I had a boyfriend, and if the boyfriend would mind those hours? I remember thinking 'What a cheek!' How he would never ask a man that question. He was right, though. Not many guys expect their girls to be working in the evenings. They set up a battle for her loyalties. I remember deciding it would help sort the sheep from the goats, sift out the ones who saw women as equals with a right to an interesting job. My rule of thumb did not always work! Anyway, what if traditionally a woman's loyalties were to her man and children first? Does the non-traditional woman give hers to her job first? Does that bring her any more satisfaction? I've often said I need a wife, not a husband!

ME I noticed a lot of things about working with men, too! I'd gone straight into a very male job, working as a sub-editor, which means you do the lay-out of the pages in the editorial section, but you also work with the printers, seeing the page through into the printed form. Printers are a closed shop. It's work for men only. But they will work with female subs, happily if they're pretty. When I first went to work in the composing room of the newspaper, with a hundred or so men, it was still the days of the mini-skirt and the bra-less look. Men, and especially printers, are not shy about telling you what they see, what they like and how you look. I played into their hands, I know, by dressing that way. But one half of me thought, 'Why should I compromise the way I dress for a false sense of prudery? Just so I don't get a bad name?' The other half of me enjoyed the undercurrents of sex anyway.

At the same time as they were saying they liked working with me, were they thinking I was a slut? When they whistled and made the odd crude noise, were they despising me for letting them get away with it? If I laughed along at their crude jokes, was that bad form? There were times when it got downright exhausting. Every day the same old comments. Every day someone discussing what I was wearing. It was all two-sided. I could have avoided the trouble by down-playing the way I projected myself. But then I wouldn't have had half so much fun! I loved working with them – the banter and humour, the basic earthy quality of their conversations. I liked the fact it was the old game of males and females, playing at the working game. We weren't just cogs in the factory wheel.

But – and there is another 'but'. I know I only got on well with the printers because I was happy to play the role that one of us prescribed (I'm not sure which) of the 'little girl'. The easiest way to get on with men you don't really relate to, is to play the little girl. Obviously, they don't feel threatened by you and they know how to relate to you too in that role. So I was the little girl to them. Smiling, taking the jokes, looking happy. I was pleased to act it out. I was the princess, the little lady. Sometimes I'd get caught when friends visited if they knew me in another context. They'd say 'Why do you act so childish?' I didn't know then that I just have lots of roles that I play out in my life. I'm never really quite sure, from day to day, which is the real me.

The trouble with my little girl role was it carried over into life among my colleagues. I used to say to my friends, or boyfriends, in despair, that I'd never be able to get on in that career as I could not grow up. I'd set my role as the young, carefree, careless girl. And I didn't know how to mature without leaving that parental background. It was my failing, not theirs. There are lots of women who have managed it better than I have. But I didn't want to copy them either. The role of the serious, smart, sophisticated career woman didn't seem any more appealing, no more *me*. It's like what Georgina said about being eighteen and wondering which pattern of female life to copy. There never seems one that fits!

HEATHER I realize too I am actually a mass of contradictions. My life is turning out so that I'm acting the part that used to be played by men. In so far as I have relationships that allow me to express different sides of myself, they are all equally important to me. Yet I can see relationships developing with people who have no idea of my other sides. I've got my different roles. Which is the real me? I don't know. I've always followed my own nose, even as far as doing something for a living. I've maybe tried too hard to identify with things I do. Or with people I know. So when it stops meaning anything I have to get out of whatever it is.

GEORGINA The career women in TV dress well, in refined, sophisticated, toning clothes, and keep that air of mystery – no man would ever comment on their nipples! I know just what you mean. They are taken seriously, on politics or pollution, and they get promotions. Being a carefree girl doesn't get me promotions either, though I suppose I'm growing out of it now. I've smartened up now, I feel I'm here to stay.

Maybe part of me was frightened before of being classed in the career-woman role. Being the carefree type meant I was working but still available to men. Or maybe I didn't really want to be held back by the straitjacket of a traditional career. It certainly wasn't the life of adventures I was looking for. Early on, I began to get bored and stale, wondering if I would stay in the safe job, with a pension, till I was sixty? To stop myself feeling a sell-out, I had to carry on laughing, playing the fool, not taking work seriously. I had to wear outrageous clothes that I hoped did not conform. I don't think women should be taken so literally at face value. But even so, I was surprised to hear a comment from one of my ex-bosses. He could not understand why I acted like an 'office girl'. Didn't he understand it was more fun to act the office girl, knowing you had a serious mind behind it? How would a man have had to act to get a similar comment?

POLLY I loved all the status and glamour when I first went to work. It seemed very adult and exciting. Having lived with Mick for nearly three years, I was very complacent. I knew what men and marriage were all about. Then I was thrust into this exciting world, full of older, interesting men who treated me as an equal and chatted me up in the pub. Men like P.G. who commissioned the latest political books. He was a star. Not only a star in my eyes, but in everyone else's. That was important. So I did my best to get off with him. It meant I was seen to be, up to a point, with a star man. That little pathetic me, at twenty-two, just out of university, with no great self confidence, was fancied by the cream of that company. It was a great boost. The fact that I pleased him, that was my myth. It's important to please your man in bed, I know, but I made it into, 'I'm all right in bed because I can please someone like P.G.' It's a very masochistic, self-negating trip that one. It meant, 'I exist because of him; I am sexy because he finds me sexy.' Not because I find myself sexy.

GEORGINA Are you sure you didn't really do it for a better job?

POLLY Oh no. My career wasn't that important. I didn't have a clear sense of what I wanted to do. After being in the job for a year, a new fantasy began which was that I got into the world of politics. It was trendy and I wanted to get into the main stream of political editing, under P.G. of course. I started to send in ideas to him. Suddenly it was very appealing that this door was open to me, that I could become one of those gritty, tough political women. But I only wanted to do it because that's what P.G. and his kind were. They were the most interesting men around – the stars.

In the end, I left Mick and moved in with Damon. Not that I wanted him but because I wanted to be more a part of the publishing scene. There were all these top people around to be fancied. It was a dreadfully incestuous place. It was the glamour – it convinced *me* I was someone. But I knew that. We all did, didn't we? – that a part of us got off on the power thing and a part of us cringed because really we were still 'little me'. I did six months with the political section, half way up the ladder. It was obvious I wasn't interested in current affairs or politics. I had to face the hard and bitter fact that I never even read the papers! I found them really boring! I didn't want to sit and read about what goes on in the Middle East or Ireland, or what Marx said – then. Now I'm changing back that way again.

GEORGINA Power is sexy. Power does attract, doesn't it? I find that, being emotional, women are in love with their jobs if they half way like them; in love with the city or country they live in too. So it often makes sense to have an affair, to be in love, with a man who is part of that area of emotion. If a man likes your work you love him. If he helps you on your way you love him. If he wants your body you'll love him even more. I've always been emotional about my work. But power also attracts because it makes the man seem superior and dominant even if his personality is not. And power attracts because some of it may rub off on you. And all those qualities added together make the sum of good sex – for a while, don't they? Afterwards? Well, it tends to be back to the old sordid story we were warned about in women's magazines. One of you has to get out. The weaker one goes to the wall. But a girl knows she's only a passenger, not stopping to get hurt.

Bringing our feelings to work of course has been the biggest obstacle to women getting on in the world of men. You still get jokes about women executives taking breaks for crying, about women not being able to be politicians because they suffer pre-menstrual tension and might make the wrong decisions. The guys who make the jokes completely forget their own variable moods and emotions, and it doesn't cross their minds that their repressed emotions might lead to worse decisions. One girl researcher I worked with got so fed up with the cameramen teasing her that she burst into tears in front of them. They were ever so shocked. Yet they are never shocked when a man gets angry. Men make rude remarks about women suffering their menopause, about women having periods and being crabby. It's a man's world in the professions. If we want to come in and join them, we're supposed to be surrogate men, behave like men, wear Tampax, take the Pill, never suffer any emotions, and take their values as our own too! There are times when as a girl, working with men, I *hate* them.

9 That's not liberation

GEORGINA Ah, but there was a thin line that nobody crossed at that time. When we were girl students, the first generation of the bulge, who had been allowed access to education, and had flocked to universities *en masse*, everything was fine for us. We felt we were getting the best of both worlds. We were having fun. We could be sexy and academic at the same time. We were in a man's world and loving it. Why should we care about the so-called problems of women? On that level, I only remember when I was reading American Studies we read Willa Cather in the literature part. I dutifully took down in my notes that Willa Cather was a good writer, though a lady, because there was a 'male strength' to her prose. Nothing female or wishy-washy or sentimental about Willa. I hadn't had it pointed out to me, that very few writers on university courses were women. That we were in fact studying the fruits of male culture. But even Germaine Greer had not been heard then. When it was first whispered, none of us went running to greet the new Women's Movement with open arms, did we? We were scared stiff of it. Some women still are. To accept it puts you outside the man's world, puts you beyond the pale for individual men. And it can be very lonely out there.

I got involved to some degree at work – at least, my name became associated with Women's Liberation. But never really. Just like in 1968 with lefty politics. I'm not a joiner of groups. I did notice the women in television were rather frightened of coming together in the early days, around 1972, in case they looked as if they were slipping back into the traditional female world by doing so. A group of women talking together, even high-powered professional women, still got the comments about 'wittering' and 'gossiping'. But there was one subject that always drew women, even the competitive ones, together. That is when they start talking about their contraception failures, problems and pains. As I say that, I can just imagine the kind of reaction it would get from the men in my office! Laughter, scorn, contempt, boredom? As if it's being old-fashioned to talk about such things and not to be the modern, streamlined, period-free, non-emotional women, they want as their colleagues. Anyway, we do get premenstrual tension and bad periods at work. Most of us have controlled the system to fit our life-styles by now. But you can still get caught out and when you do, you don't feel like smiling.

The day I came out of hospital having had a coil fitted, I went straight back to the office. I'd had it fitted at the suggestion of a doctor in the hospital, who told me I was being stupid not to let him experiment with other Pills till I found the right one for me. 'What's the proof?' I said, 'My death?' remembering what had happened to Carol. (Actually I didn't say that although I did think about it.) He put that coil in though, and I screamed the place down. It was a Lippes Loop, before the days of the Copper 7. He told me it should be all right. I lay on the trolley with my feet in stirrups and let him torture me. When it was inserted through the cervix, my body went into a state of spasm. I blacked out with the pain, lurched and drew up my feet. 'What's wrong?' he said crossly. 'Shall I take it out?' I didn't, couldn't, reply. He took it out and put another in. 'You shouldn't be so tense,' he said. 'I wasn't tense,' I replied tensely. 'Move along, please,' said the nurse, bustling me off. I was in a state of shock by then, unable even to walk. No cup of tea, no soothing voice. 'What about the pain? Is it bad?' she said brusquely. 'Excruciating.' 'Take Panadol.' I lived on Panadol for nine months. I lived on Tampax too. I bled for weeks. Ten-day periods, mid-term bleeds, overdue periods, pains that recurred without warning in the morning, the evening, any time. It began to make me feel old. It was a very effective contraceptive! Poor Robert had to suffer it all too. Looking back, it was just after my abortion. I'm sure my uterus was rejecting the coil. Unfortunately, the doctor I went to complain to said that I over-reacted. He phrased it, 'You really want a baby.' My hackles rose. How dare he try to put me in the slot with all other women? Male chauvinist, him. But he could have explained it better. Those kind of contraceptive methods are all so unnatural.

Anyway, during my time of suffering, none of those men in the office knew what I was going through. You don't go in and say 'I may be crabby today because I'm in agony, bleeding, living from Panadol to Panadol. And if my eyes glaze over it's because I'm trying to work out if I've soaked through the Tampax, or whether that's nervous sweat? OK? You go into work and have to be bright, smiley and flirtatious, take the jibes against women, and all the time you're smouldering, thinking, 'None of you goes through this. Why is it all so unfairly weighted?'

I used to get really upset too, when I first started work, to notice that only the older women had children. Younger women were all putting off the day, not sure when to embark on that very different career of motherhood. That's why I still find the life-style we've chosen confusing. It obviously isn't natural. Quite a few have begun to have their babies now they're in their early thirties. I haven't managed it yet. I still don't know how to take the plunge.

One day, one of the guys in the newsroom walked in with a large cuddly toy, and put it by his typewriter. It was a white fluffy dog, almost the size of a three year-old. I asked him what it was. 'Oh, I'm taking it home for my boy. It's his birthday.' I know I felt like crying there and then. This man, or any of the men who worked there, could combine his career with his family because he had a woman at home who had given up her career to have the children. The women in television, the bright young women, would never be able to pursue their careers so selfishly *and* have children. One day they might have a baby. But, from that day on, they would be out of the game really – out of the pursuit of prestige, money, glamour, fun, travel and adventure. Maybe they're right!

HEATHER Yes, but none of the women I knew, or know now, ever went to any consciousness raising groups. I never felt that it was worth it, to sit in a room with ten or so other women moaning about men. Polly, you, me and Georgina knew each other well enough to talk about our deepest thoughts anyway.

POLLY I never wanted to know about all the Women's Liberation stuff. To me, they were off on the wrong tack. I was much more into the world where men and women learned to weave, sew, grow organic food, make things, have families. Those Liberation women seemed very fucked up to me. I like being a woman. New Age women are very traditional really. Mind you, I have just met a guy who doesn't fit into my prescribed formula – the ideal image I was looking for. And I've suddenly found myself reading Germaine Greer – seven years late, isn't it? More of a way of finding out what he might be into, than for my own sake.

GEORGINA I should think so too, Polly. It's interesting when you talk about men, you actually *sound* the most feminist of us all. You use the phraseology. You talk about your fear of men dominating you.

POLLY But it's deeper than Women's Lib stuff. One of my biggest problems with men was always that I'd swamp myself totally in their identity, turn into a snivelling, pathetic little being who wasn't interested in anything of her own, only in the guy's world, and whatever was divine and wonderful about him – obviously he wasn't really divine and wonderful – I couldn't handle. Whatever it was, anyway, came from me. I projected it on to him. If you're going out with a god, you're always inadequate, always a nothing. You can never be equal with him.

It happened sexually too. Because I pushed all the identity on to him, I spent all that time worrying whether I was pleasing him in bed, and never worked out about me. In all those years in my twenties, I never went with a man I didn't feel inadequate with. Now that I've worked on my own creative energy, now that I've got into therapy, I am finding out who *I* am. At the moment, I've got the reverse situation, I feel superior to them! Like with Zed. To begin with I laid that divine trip on him, then, after the infatuation, I found I didn't like him very much. His self-sufficiency, his air of mystery, was something I wanted at first. But he was too fucked up. There've been three others since Zed I've broken with. One, I put a divine trip on again. And the third, right now, I'm just beginning to approach as another human being with similar problems to my own. I'm definitely into *my* problems now. No man is ever going to take me over, make me lose my identity again. Of course, they will do. But at least I'm on the way. I've found my work, my weaving, I know there is something creative in me. I may produce something nice one day!

GEORGINA It's funny that you don't come over at all as inadequate with us – just with men. Do you think you have very deep-rooted fears about your 'femaleness'? I only ask because I'm working that one out about myself right now. After all these years of being the bold, raunchy girl, Martin came along – very much the male to my female – and out it all came again; the fears, the feelings of inadequacy. I realize I must have a lot of very deep fears about my femininity. Sometimes I really think I've got no femaleness at all.

POLLY Let me tell you a dream I had the other night. I was with my brother and, like Victorian teenage children, we were being sold as servants. A Victorian gentleman came along and said to the man selling us, 'You'd do better to sell the boy on his own. On his own he's worth more than the couple.' So, the girl's presence belittles the boy. Which meant – Christ – I don't think much of myself. Then I was left standing on a railway station with nowhere to go. I couldn't go home and I hadn't been sold. That's when Zed appeared on the platform and in the dream I watched myself hesitating between going to join him or not. He must have stood for a one last final, false, sense of freedom.

GEORGINA Do you think we fear our femininity because of the social thing? You know, the conditioning argument – that it was the way we were brought up? Because we didn't conform to what was feminine even at school? We were clever, therefore we could not be feminine and pretty? It meant we were outsiders in a female world? Or what is a woman anyway? Maybe it's because we haven't had any children that deep down we fear we are absolutely useless?

POLLY I don't believe in all that. We may have been clever at school but we certainly weren't bluestockings. We went out with virile lads, not pathetic little boys. I don't think about the social conditions, only about *my* condition. I think the extreme feminists are probably very confused about their roles as women. And that's probably because they haven't resolved problems with their parents.

You know when it became fashionable to call ourselves 'women' instead of 'girls', I used to have to swallow really hard. I felt a complete fraud calling myself a 'woman'.

GEORGINA And me! You notice I still refer to myself as a 'girl', or, as guys say these days, 'lady'. And here am I, thirty! But Polly, I still think you're the least frightened of us. You're not bothered by being thirty and single, are you?

POLLY I am an optimist. Which links with being thirty. To me, thirty was always a great ideal. I'd be seen as a person. Now I know I don't have to conform to any one life-style. I can be *me*. I can eat white rice with the macro freaks if I want to!

HEATHER You know, looking back, I think all through my twenties I would have married at the drop of a hat if I'd met the fantasy person. The fantasy was what was left over from my childhood. I was brought up to see the *man* as the person who would express things for me. I was brought up to see myself married to someone creative and trendy, so I could become that and express my creativity through him. I grew up expecting that. Expecting someone I'd instantly worship. But I didn't allow for the fact I would become a discriminating person through the freedom of shopping around and widening my own horizons. So that when these men came along I didn't recognize them because they weren't enough any more. My having an equal say in the relationship wasn't right to them. And it was at times like that, I'd wake up in the morning and think, 'Ugh, who is this person?' And kick him out. Or else, I fell flat on my face for the person who wouldn't let me do that. So I thought he was this fantasy strong man because he was being strong as far as I was concerned. That's what you're talking about, Polly. Every man I knew fell into those extremes. The shits or the softies.

POLLY Yes, I often wonder what they were expecting from us that we didn't give them?

GEORGINA That's what I meant about no man really wanting to be with someone like us. They want a woman who is lively and interesting. Oh yes. But not really a self-motivated person.

HEATHER We're very different, you and I, Georgina. Your independence is something you developed through a relationship. Mine was by default.

GEORGINA You were quite a masochist in relationships, though, weren't you? I'm the opposite. Men have always seen me as selfish.

HEATHER I don't know. I suppose I'm free, because the person never came along, to say I'd have married at the drop of a hat in my twenties – I have no reason to doubt it! All I did was have relationships that went wrong! (*laughter*) – Or not have relationships and have to compensate in some way. That's how I developed my independence. Because I knew if I waited for a man to be there before I did things, I ended up not doing anything. (*laughter*) – I still find I'm in a weird situation because everyone's emotional allegiance is to the other half of a couple. If you're a well-adjusted single person, you're not half as emotionally secure as those in couples. Because you can't rely on anyone to that extent. I suppose I got to the point in the last few years where no-one really knew *me* because no-one had that day to day living thing with me.

GEORGINA How long is it now, you've been single like this?

HEATHER 'Single like this' – it sounds like the title of a bad novel! I suppose nearly three years. Don't say that! Somehow, in that period, I got into relationships with older men instead, platonic relationships. But anyway, I woke up one day in my late twenties to accept I was living on my own. Not, as in my dream, with a man. I hadn't had a long-term relationship in years, after Tom or Benny. I had some rethinking to do, in terms of how my family saw me, and of my own expectations, and in terms of how men, or society saw me. I had to learn not to sit at home in misery being a single woman but that my own friendships with men or women were valuable, that my own way of life had merit. It's a struggle, in this couple orientated society, and I suppose it always will be. And of course the more independent you are the more you like it that way.

That's how I came to meet the ideas of the Women's Movement half way. I'd never ever thought of myself as the feminist type. I'm the old-fashioned, traditional type of woman ...

GEORGINA Why do you say I learned my independence through a relationship? You mean from Robert? I don't see it that way. I learned because I was interested in all the ideas around at the time, because in TV and the media, people pick up any new ideas and use them. Somehow, as a young female TV researcher, I *had* to decide which side I was on and to join in.

ME Same for me. I honestly don't know whether I began to write about ideas loosely connected with the Women's Movement because I was a young woman searching for an identity in a profession, or whether I felt really driven to it. I did it because it was there.

GEORGINA It's affected our lives now, though, hasn't it? We can never be the sweet, retiring, demure young women we were brought up to be. Never ever.

ME Rosie Boycott came round to see me when I was a newcomer

to London. She and Marsha Rowe were setting up *Spare Rib*, with all the energy and fanaticism necessary to launch a new baby off the ground, against opposition, and with no money. Rosie and Marsha were daring. They were also frightening to someone like me from the provinces. They seemed attractive, courageous, ballsy and very threatening; part of that London mafia, the super-trendies, who had brought out *It* and *Ink* in the alternative society days. They had groovy flats and groovy friends, I thought. I didn't see them as *my* sisters. Heather, Polly and Georgina were that. When Rosie first mentioned *Spare Rib*, I can remember my reactions. On the one hand, here was a new and exciting magazine, and heaven knows anyone would want to be part of it. On the other, it meant commitment to a way-out philosophy which might stamp my own passport with the wrong sort of visa. I was a coward. But I was scared of being numbered among the feminists. Would anyone else ever want me to work for them then? I was living with a guy, Pete, at the time and I wailed to him that I was frightened, that I was sure they were a bunch of lesbians, that I didn't want to end up like that.

Sisterhood? Their version – not *Spare Rib*'s but the kind being talked about in general – didn't mean much to me. I'd grown up with my girlfriends. We had learned not to be competitive with each other. We poured our souls out to each other, regularly, with no trouble. So what did this new sisterhood mean?

During that first year, 1972, I became quite convinced that I must be lesbian after all. My dreams were obsessed with fantasies about what sleeping with another woman would be like. I remember one hot summer day, interviewing an American woman writer about her feminist-type book. She was one of those warm, emotional, very sensitive women with whom I was immediately at ease. I fantasized while I was talking to her that at the evening reception to launch her book, our eyes would meet across the room, and with no effort at all, I'd be drawn towards her. We'd float off out of the room and fall in a pile of coats, disappearing into each other's arms and – love. Then my fantasy blacked out. I was much too scared of homosexual love to get involved.

But I cried one day when I felt that's what had to be. I wondered how I'd tell my parents. How I'd face up to the social disgrace, imagining people whispering 'Carol's queer, you know.' It had been hard enough writing to tell my parents that Pete and I were living together and weren't going to get married. But then that was all bravado, part of the ethics of our age. I could no more have gone against my own need to be unconventional, by marrying, than I could have gone along with their wish to see me neatly parcelled off as a Mrs. My parents took it quite happily. They'd read about such things in the papers, seen it all on TV.

My own views about women and the need for the Women's Movement only began to come clear when I embarked on a project with an Australian girl, who was not one of my old friends, but the girl who was living with one of Pete's friends. It was a challenge for me to do something with another woman – yes, Polly, that's when we started to try and use the word 'woman'! She and I had to learn to work together, to learn what we had to offer each other and why.

The project was good, and for me a turning point. We decided to research language, from a sexist viewpoint. It was a revelation and an eye-opener to me. There was something after all, behind the talk about the great hype against women. We used to take the dictionary, letter by letter, sifting through for sexist definitions of words, for words that had acquired sexist connotations. We took Shakespeare and found him riddled with abusive, usually sexually abusive, sexist words, and we looked through proverbs and famous sayings. The evidence mounted. My two favourites, not to give the whole game away, are: 'Strong-minded – having such mind, also and usually in special sense of women, claiming mental and legal equality with men.' We would roar with laughter at such juicy finds, loving the lexicographer's patronizing use of the word 'claiming'. The other one was: 'Slut – slovenly woman, slattern, (joc.) girl.' We found out that the word was derived from the Anglo-Saxon word 'sloven'. 'Sloven' was the male form and came to mean simply dirty, untidy, unkempt. 'Slut' was the female form, taking a sexual connotation, because, we all know, that a slut is someone who is sexually casual as well as sloppily dressed! In fact evidence of male anger at women's sexuality was so strong we got quite scared. Did they really feel so hostile to women who were free?

For the two of us working at our project, it had become part of the need to stake out our new female territory. We would meet on Saturday afternoons and sometimes one other afternoon in the week. It was meant to be part of that new consciousness of women meeting together to do something constructive, but really it was a bit forced. In some ways it felt no higher in its consciousness than if we were two suburban housewives meeting to play bridge in the afternoons. As intellectual, thinking young women we were aware of the anomalies, and were made even angrier by them. She used to get upset that, in fact, I was closer to my other friends. We both knew that we were being competitive with each other. Put to the test we weren't really friends.

GEORGINA Oh God, yes. I remember one of my worst failures was when I tried to set up a programme to be called 'Women as friends'. It was one of those things that would not come right, so it never got made. I intended to have a group of women in the studio talking about friendship, so we could sort out the lie that only men have true friends and women are always jealous and competitive with each other. The trouble was *me*. I was trying to re-evaluate Polly's and Heather's friendship. We were finding each other in a new way after all those years of growing up together, exploring a new kind of friendship to take us into the next decade. Something a bit more than just gossiping and backing each other up. I thought I was being *so* liberated. But I was just corny. I was still being Robert's 'little woman'. And it was because of me that the tone of the programme went all wrong.

Now that I'm living on my own I'm much more friendly with both of you again. But I also realize I'm not playing a game now. We'll probably stick together through life.

HEATHER I hope not. I'm sick of you all! (*laughter*) Actually, Georgina, you really are the most *un*liberated girl I know.

ME I had the same paradox. The me who was spouting all these ideas in print was living a completely different life in reality. Pete was a rock climber and he introduced me to an extremely male way of life which I loved. It was carefree, and careless – lots of drinking, parties, rock music – and who cares about work, careers, or even money? They modelled themselves on James Dean, Ken Kesey, the Merry Pranksters – Hell's Piss Artists. I couldn't have lived all that without men. They had fun. There was a whole group of girls going around with climbers who did not want to know anything about Women's Lib or such London orientated things. They were liberated in that other way. They weren't married and didn't have children. They didn't have to be terribly feminine. Instead they could enjoy sleeping rough, travelling light, drinking hard, and spending the money you could earn then on the new goodies – stereos, cars, long trips abroad. It was a freedom with no particular problems. Except it's hard to change from that way of life.

GEORGINA Women are the world's worst critics of another woman's man, aren't they? You feel all eyes upon you as a failure for only being able to *get* a man if you're seen dragging a drunk home! Robert drank a lot and smoked a lot and I understood why he did it. Most of my men have. Men can never talk about their confusions and crises like we can. They just drown themselves in drugs instead. Some guys drank, smoked, got up to all the evils of the modern world, because it showed courage and daring, showed us they were men. It usually meant they were sexually adventurous too. Which I liked!

A lot of my times with Robert were very funny. But the early 70s divided everything into male and female, instead of one human being with another. Robert understood women and liked them. He was contemporary, liberated in the way men of our age are. We came together as equals and that's how we struggled on, day by day. I'm not really the domesticated type. I didn't want to be the housewife to the husband. But I suppose I did expect him to do the male things like arrange to decorate the flat, and know how to fix a leaking toilet. As for our domestic routine, I think I expected he would go into it with me. He didn't.

I remember feeling really peeved, after only a few weeks together, that I made the bloody bed every day. It wasn't that I wouldn't make my own bed if I lived on my own, it was that *he* was getting away without having to make *his* bed any more just by living with me. We worked different hours and I was at home more in the shopping hours, so he expected me to get the food and cook our evening meal every day. He was working-class really and I know, in his heart of hearts, he wanted to be able to come back and find his tea on the table. 'Where's mi tea?' he would say, putting on his Northern accent, and I'd bristle and say 'What tea? Have you made it?'

We'd argue over who emptied the rubbish bins, over who went to the launderette, and who would clean up the flat. After a year or two I gave up and started to clean the place as if it was my own. That's when I realized I wanted to live on my own. He started to do the launderette then and would proclaim himself liberated in public because he did that! I sound awful. I don't know any couple who works it out well.

Our funniest scenes, I think, were when I was at work. I was there early evenings a lot. I'd get a phone call from him. If you could have seen me in that mixed open office, you'd have laughed. At first I'd be pleased to hear his voice and I'd say 'Hello, what's going on?' Then my face would freeze and I'd turn my back on the other people, knowing I had to whisper and speak through gritted teeth. He would be saying 'What's to eat tonight?' angrily, after a couple of years of it. And I'd say, with pretend sweetness, 'There's eggs and cheese in the fridge, you can make something to eat, can't you?' He'd say 'You know I can't get to the shops, and that I need a meal.' All the indignation in the world would rise up in me, as I'd look at myself in that office, holding down a professional job, and I'd be thinking 'What am I doing with a man ringing *me* up asking where *his* meal is?' Down went the phone.

I think I must be the original Shrew. Women's Lib was great for stroppy bitches like myself! I used to think men liked the battle. Maybe they don't! Oh help! (*laughter*)

ME So where did Women's Liberation get us in real life? I often used to wonder what Gloria Steinem and Germaine Greer did in the nitty-gritty of everyday life? What were their household arguments like?

HEATHER It seems to me now that in recent years women have put about a new myth – which is that all men are bastards, all men are wrong. What we've been doing is creating some new fantasy male who will miraculously fit the blueprint we've designed for the new 'liberated' male. But in fact it's as much myth. Why should they fit our way of thinking?

ME The real test for me came when Pete and I split up. I'd

spent the whole of the second half of my twenties with him. So where did it leave me once I was on my own? I do realize that I was only able to get so involved, be so outspoken, because of the paradox that I was living with him. He bolstered my liberated stance. Since he's been gone and I've been on my own, I've found I'm a lot less sure of myself.

GEORGINA The other night, when Heather suggested we went to a pub theatre together, I jumped at the idea – until she said it would have to be a Saturday night. It was a pub I used to go to with Robert, I knew his friends would be there, and I was going to be embarrassed being seen going to the theatre on a Saturday night with a girlfriend! So much for the liberated me. I think it's because Saturday night is traditionally a night for getting your rocks off. It's tame to be two women at the theatre.

But we still are a muddle of confusions aren't we. We *know* we should not need men for social conformity, but it's bloody hard not to lean on them for that. Through all my liberated years, too, I had a man to go to parties with, to go to dinners with, to go home to after political meetings! I don't even know what I believe in. Is there any point in the end in learning to live without men? Why would I be a better person if I was happy to be spending Saturday night with a girlfriend?

10 Now we are thirty

GEORGINA We are single and we've passed thirty. We haven't had any children and we're obsessed by the question of whether we will or not. That about sums us up, doesn't it? The only thing that is reassuring is that in London, and other major cities in the Western world, there seem to be an awful lot of women like us. You only have to go twenty miles outside the metropolitan area though, and you feel as if you are wearing a funny hat with a big red S on it – for Spinster, don't you?

ME The road we travelled has left us with a unique view of life though, that cannot change now. Lots of things have happened because of the turns we took on the way. I sometimes feel that, in my attitudes and general level of responsibility, the me at thirty is how the teenager imagined I would be at twenty-five. One simple example – I wear a bra now! I'd hate to wander round with my nipples showing for labourers and bus drivers to see. And I have a sneaking sadness that small though they may be, my tits have dropped because of those braless years.

POLLY I don't feel that I have the same identity crises that lots of women coming out of early marriages suffer, because I have devoted the last eight or nine years to carving away at just that.

GEORGINA Since being on my own though, I laugh to realize one area I lack identity in is music. My taste in music seems to have gone from soul (me as a teenager), to classical music (Martin), to progressive rock and laid-back Californian groups (Robert) and back to soul music (West Indian boyfriend). I like women's singing, like Carly Simon, and Aretha Franklin, because they sing about feelings and emotions I share. I like all that other music too, but I tend to listen to it in men's company. Similarly, I like women's books and paintings.

HEATHER I've lived in all sorts of ways. In my student days, I used to have my own flat. It was me who took the leases and organized everything. For a while, when I was working professionally, I had my own cottage in the country. But it went with the job so I lost it. I've lived in the caravan. I've shared houses. For four years I was one member of a large communal flat. It was fine at first, it replaced family for each other. We had a routine of cooking and cleaning and that left you lots of time free. But for the last couple of years I've felt very isolated. They weren't family. In the end, we were strangers who didn't care about each other. So I've moved to a smaller flat now, which I share with a couple of others, and which is more like mine. I'm a leaseholder again. But it's still like student life.

I'd found that any time I leant on a guy who I was sleeping with, he backed away. So I found instead I was developing some nice non-sexual relationships. I had three older men like that. One in his 40s, and two in their 50s. They gave me something I wanted. They'd call for me in taxis, take me out for dinner, buy me presents, walk on the outside of me, open doors. They were the kind of man I'd been brought up to marry. I'd never experienced all that. From our student days, we were paying our way as equals. I suddenly experienced this incredible feeling of being taken care of and I felt that's what I needed. I still have a relationship with one guy in his 50s. And now I've a physical relationship with Rick. The only thing that holds me back in keeping up all these multiple relationships is the thought of getting pregnant.

I've always been a loner. I don't invite people back to where I live because I haven't got a double bed! But it's a convenient excuse. I can control when I get rid of them by the fact that it's me who leaves.

People used to act parts, now there are no rules left, no set procedure. It seems to be totally arbitrary as to how your life develops. Depending on what type of person makes the bigger demand on you first. For example, Charles, the older guy, is talking about buying a house and setting up a community with several people. And I agree with the idea, because I couldn't cope with living as a couple! I talk about marriage but I don't know how much that is ... (*silence*) ... It's finally happened – I've dried up! (*laughter*)

ME Why can't you live as a couple?

HEATHER It's the difference between the fantasy and the reality. Because I've been in a situation again, since knowing Rick, where I could consider living that way; because I've thought about it, I am going back to all those old values. You really have to know someone, be sure of a lot of things, before you live with them. You really have to be prepared to work at the relationship. And I'm only interested in what's real for me. Life's too short and all that. What is all this pairing off thing? Ultimately it's like wrapping yourself in cotton wool and saying goodbye to a part of your own identity. Being with one other person, you do stop doing your own thing. I haven't done any of my painting recently, because of Rick. He absorbs a whole part of me. I have to face up to that. If I was to live in a one-to-one thing again, I would have to compromise.

POLLY Oh no. When we get down to it, what I want is very conventional. It's husbands and wives living in houses, in country villages, working hard for their living, having kids. Maybe what they're doing looks a little more unconventional to the housewives in Surbiton because they're mending wagons, not cars. But in that way we can get out of our paradox of being conventional and unconventional at the same time.

The trouble with me is I'm in danger of setting up another fantasy image – about the New Age culture this time. The image is that I'm the sort of person who goes with travelling groups and sits on the sea shore round bonfires, plays drums and eats brown rice. Just like the 'I'm a glamorous publishing girl' one. I'm using it in the same way too, to prop myself up. What I'm trying to do is get in touch with me.

That's why I got into therapy in the end. My brother was in analysis and I knew I needed some form of help. I felt I wasn't looking at something running up behind me and tapping me on the shoulder. In the end, you know, I've only taken up the therapy because I want a husband and children and some work that is fulfilling. I've found my work now – my weaving. But as for men, well . . . When I met a man, if he didn't fit, then I thought 'Let's get out of this, this isn't the perfect man.' I knew it was up to me to change and I actually needed a guiding hand.

HEATHER I realized, like Polly, rather late that I wanted some creative pursuit. I did all that teaching thing for years, then ultimately felt *I* wasn't getting anything out of it. I'd done some freelance work, and in the end took up pottery and some painting. I started to work as a typist or secretary so I could spend the rest of my time going to drawing classes, going back to the drawing I used to do as a teenager. I've been doing it for four or five years now, without much success, though sometimes I feel as if I'm getting somewhere. It was that day when I realized there wasn't going to be one man who would fill all the gaps in my life. I had to find some other way of expressing *me*.

ME But which is the real person? I know I have a repertoire of roles I act out with the different people I know. I can play cutesy girl, sophisticated city girl, cynical vamp, worldly wise wit, bitch, charming middle-class girl, responsible or cultured woman, mother to many men, sister to others, clinging wreck to one, friend to most women, in awe of some, threatened by others, bored by many, and strange alien creature to most children. Though I want them to see me as the sort of wayward, bachelor elder sister figure.

I don't really know what my life-style is. I quite enjoy being single, I realize that. Sometimes I feel that to live with a man again would only constrain my life-style, limit me, alter my sense of identity. Other times, I just accept I'm in limbo waiting for another man to come along to make form and substance out of it all. Although I have my own routine and feel I know my inner self, I'm sure I leave at least forty of the three hundred and sixty degrees that are me open to be given to the man I choose.

As for the life-style, it's still the social life that is hardest for a woman alone. I have friends from work, friends from when I was part of a couple, my girlfriends, some men friends. I have my own place which gives me a tremendous feeling of security, of space, of the fact of my existence. At the same time, I shout at it sometimes to go away as it's my 'trap'! Here am I set up in my singleness and I feel the house is setting me in that mould. It will hold me that way.

GEORGINA You lot keep telling me I'm the career woman now, just because I've stayed in my job and have money. But I just see it that I need the work and the money to hold me together. I couldn't survive as Heather and Polly do, with little cash, no security whatsoever. Not even as a freelance. I do enjoy being professional and getting respect from other people – I have to admit it. But I am frightened of the career-woman tag! I suppose it conjures up someone who is cold, sorted out, who has put her career before her emotional life. But it's not like that, is it? For this whole year I've been an emotional wreck. My job has been the one thing that has held me together.

ME When I went freelance, which meant working at home, the one thing I was concerned about was that I didn't end up feeling like a housewife! Yet sometimes I wonder why the hell I spend the whole day on the typewriter. Is it to fill time because I haven't got children to look after and work around the house to do? I need the money. But it's like Heather says, we opted for the creative expression rather than going for self-expression through raising children. I told myself I'd never do anything more than washing up on weekdays. I could clean the house like any working girl at weekends. I was frightened of being associated with bored housewives.

GEORGINA Ellie comes to visit me with her three children. She's at the stage of wondering how to carve out a career now. She's the other end of the spectrum. I look at her girls, the eldest is ten, and I think what has my life to show for itself in the same way? Children are still a fantasy I play with. Not pregnant, I can dream of what it would be like, work out how to fit caring for a child into my life. Yet I know that the day I was pregnant, the fantasy vanished and reality sprang all too quickly into place. The day I was pregnant all my old fears flooded back.

'Why have a child now?' my inner voice says. 'Do you want to spoil the way of life you have now? Lose that freedom to travel, to go out where and when you please? The freedom to spend all day doing nothing, or working intensely, with no-one to feel responsible for? What about the thought of never having a moment's privacy again? Do you want a tame life in which the domestic routine dominates?' The fantasy fades, disappears out of the window. And as I let it, the other panic wells up. The other voice says 'So you let the years slip by – 32, 34, 37? What if you get to 40 still thinking like this and find out it's too late? What will you say to yourself at 50 when you've got no children? I read the modern writers who defend not having children. But it doesn't solve the problem I face now.

ME As far as I'm concerned, my feelings of fear crystallized at thirty. Until then I was acting out the game of being brave, bold, swinging. I didn't want to marry and become a Mrs, that felt like The End. The very tag 'Mrs' felt like a nail in the coffin. By the time I'd passed thirty though, I think I caught a glimpse of the horizon on which a different age was written in large letters. Then I felt less confident. Are we being Peter Pannish? Or are we right in not tying ourselves down, leaving options and choices open?

GEORGINA I was talking with another friend recently. We were both a bit smashed. Suddenly we turned quite hysterical, hugging each other, as we admitted it's still only fantasy but it could happen that we'll always be in this state. While it seems OK even now, the idea of being forty, of having grey hairs, of still being a Miss trying to be bold as we use the term Ms, and of having other people's little children laugh at us, was terrifying. 'We'll be spinsters,' we cried. 'We'll have to commit suicide by forty!' She looked at me seriously and said, 'You know I just can't cope with the thought. It's not fair, we just aren't the *spinster* types.' Then she said 'I mean how many years do we have to go home to our parents at Christmas and pretend we're still the dutiful daughters who will do the right thing by them one day, get married and all that? It's all becoming a joke, because I realize I act that out for their sakes and mine too. Will I still pretend at 39?'

ME It hit me like that the Christmas of my thirtieth year. I was home at my parents', thinking 'What am I doing here? I'm too old to be playing the single daughter who has nowhere else to go at Christmas.' I crawled to my girlhood room during the Queen's speech and wrote a letter to the man in my life at the time. He and I were working something out, or trying to, that seemed very contemporary, without the dangers of claustrophobia. In my depression, I wrote him a long and, I thought, reasoned letter – but when I read it I could see it was hysterical. I laid out the reasons why I couldn't go on with it unless he agreed to marry me. I told him why I had to get married, because I couldn't bear what my family, their friends, people around me, would think. They would class me as a failure, a social and sexual failure, if I remained unmarried. I told him that, in the end, I could not cope with being a woman on her own.

This was *me*. A few years previously the same me had been so bold, so anti-marriage! The letter was just like one from a desperate woman of bygone years. I never posted it, of course. There's still the little worm of the conventional me that keeps wriggling its way up through the guise of the unconventional me. I think I'd still like to marry now but not for the same desperate reasons. It just seems nice now to think of committing yourself for a long time to someone, to try and build something together.

HEATHER We all still assume we have failed in the game of relationships where married members of the community haven't, don't we? In our rational moments we know better. We also know there is no such thing as success or failure, in the words of Dylan. We all choose our own particular way of living.

POLLY I get frightened too. Part of me is terrified by the age thing. Then another part says 'If I get to forty and I haven't done the family thing, then that's just the way it is.' But it's easy to sit and talk rationally. When I'm in the country scene and I'm surrounded by very together couples, by 11 p.m. the blues sink and I think 'OK, so I've got my work,' but the little voice says 'Where's the man? Why am I alone?' And I say back to it 'You know why you're alone, you've got these problems and you're working through them.' And I come back to the old despair that says 'But I'm still on my own.'

I see being independent and coping with my single life as temporary, always! (*laughter*)

I think for me to find equality with a man it's going to be a battle. It'll have to be a battleground, but that's quite healthy. As long as I don't continue feeling the inadequate little girl.

HEATHER I ought to mention my Aunt Cath. She was quite an influence on my life. All through my childhood, she was the one who came and helped out when my mother was ill. She's my mother's unmarried sister. She was always held to ridicule. She was seen to be a failure, a spinster – a sexual failure. 'Oh, Aunt Cath says there were men who wanted to marry her – ha, ha, ha.' Then I realized there was a lot I had in common with her. I started standing up for her because it meant that I was standing up for me as well. I knew I'd be the aunt who helped out. And if I don't marry, when I'm old and wrinkled I'll be saying 'Oh, there were men who wanted to marry me.' I can see she's used to living on her own and controlling her own situation. It wasn't that she didn't want to get married, just it never happened that way. She missed out on things I didn't though, because life was more repressed for her.

GEORGINA You know I split up with Robert because I was getting more involved with Martin? We even began to talk about having children. It was then I realized I couldn't go on having both of them. I'd grown out of my thing with Robert anyway. I mothered him. I organized him. In the end I wore him down. You shouldn't let a man go under you, or it's the end. We women fight like fury for control but by winning we lose out completely. Anyway, Martin came along and offered what looked like the 'real' man. I just loved it and ran into it headlong. I didn't realize I was going to have to face the other side of me. I've been acting out the daughter with him!

When Robert left my flat, Martin didn't move in. He's in television too. He's his own man, has his place and travels a lot. I thought we were going to have a very groovy existence, this glamorous roving reporter and me. But, slowly I fell to pieces. I couldn't stand my lack of control over him. I was so used to being the one in command. Now I was confronted with a very dominant man who called the tune. So, every time he went away I was a nervous wreck. I'm the classic 'little' woman with him. The kind I have learned to feel contempt for over the years. I get moody and emotionally insecure, so I'm prickly to be with, paranoid, and I should imagine utterly horrible. He's away now, and I feel better again.

When he talked about us having children, well I just fell for that. It was as if after all these years I suddenly knew I wanted them. I had the abortion before, a good five years previously. Maybe it was latent guilt but I was convinced I was sterile. I'd had a coil in for years and I decided I must be infertile. So I had it taken out when he was away on a trip. When he came back, he and I were together two weeks, but my period came. I burst into tears one morning and told him what I'd done. He left my flat and went to walk around. He phoned me half an hour later to say he thought it was wonderful and we should carry on trying to have a baby. It sounds nice, doesn't it? But – we never really talked about it. We never talked about how we'd cope when I got pregnant, or what we'd do. I didn't get pregnant and I think I felt guilty about being infertile, that I shouldn't pressure him on what may be unnecessary details. He was independent, so was I. We'd work it out.

He was away a lot over the summer, and I had a fling with another guy and thought, 'Oh what the hell – this is a lot easier than my struggle with Martin. This is what I need.' But the other guy disappeared, Martin came back for a few weeks, then had to go off again. I got pregnant. I didn't know till he had gone, though it's always on your mind if you're having sex without contraception. I was supposed to phone him and arrange to join him for a holiday. I put off phoning. Two weeks overdue and I knew what was going on. I felt sick. I got one of those quick tests done. The girl told me it was positive and said what did I want to do? I looked at her with horror. I said 'I'll have to go away and think about it.' That weekend, it was my thirtieth birthday. I spent it in a daze of thinking.

Of course I'd never thought of having an abortion. I mean I'd been trying to get pregnant. Then, as soon as I knew I'd conceived, it was as if everything fell into place. I knew I didn't really want a baby, I'd just wanted to prove I was fertile. I sat in my flat and thought everything out. It was complicated by the fact I'd been offered a better position at work, which meant more devotion to duty and a lot more energy poured in. I wanted that a lot. I wanted confirmation I was good at my job.

Then there was Martin. He was away and all my resentment for him came out. I worked out he didn't really want me, or he wouldn't be so happy travelling. He just wanted a child. So I was being used to breed for him and to mother for him. I felt invaded by his child. It seemed crystal clear. The obvious thing to do was get an abortion. I knew I could do it. The only thing against it was that I would feel embarrassed being thirty and a professional woman. I knew they would look at me and think I should have known better. I never had a moment's guilt about the idea of aborting a foetus. I just decided it was the best way to solve this mess. I'm not like you, Polly. I don't think we ought to feel pain. I never even fantasize about what the child might have been like. As far as we know, the coil might abort every month anyway.

I didn't tell Martin, give him a chance to talk it over with me or say what I felt. I just slipped right back into my old assumption that I control *my* life, I make the decisions that really concern *me*. When he eventually got through to me, I was already booked into the clinic. I lied to him about not being able to join him because of my career change. I think he sensed that somehow I was choosing career above him. I couldn't tell him because I was sure he'd talk me into having the baby. I think I was attacking him by doing it, attacking the fact he made me feel insecure and paranoid.

HEATHER But I think your emotional need is for someone who is around. He hadn't made any plans for both of you, had he?'

GEORGINA He just accepts that if I'd told him I was pregnant we'd have sorted things out from there. I feel very sad about it now. Sad that I had the abortion. Not so much that I don't have a baby now – I could get pregnant again obviously. But sad that I have this terrible fear of childbearing and at the same time this great pull towards mothering. It's nine months now, maybe that's why I feel particularly sad.

I got an abortion easily. I mean you can, can't you? I paid through one of the agencies. It was relatively cheap for a woman like me. Cheaper than bringing a human life into the world. All it meant for me was that I didn't buy so many clothes. It's amazing to hear the educated, intellectual side arguing the case for what is the emotional, biological, vulnerable side of being a woman. We really are split human beings, aren't we?

I keep wishing, looking back, that I'd done something really bizarre. I know my sense of duty had taken over at that point; I had the appointment so I had to go. I could have driven out there, and carried on driving all day, gone home and sort of kidded myself I'd had the abortion. That way I could have acted out my sensible side and let the emotional side win in a sneaky way. A nice middle-class girl like me does not do things like bring unwanted babies into the world, unmarried, or unprepared. It seems more moral for someone like me to have an abortion.

As it is, all I did was give myself another year of single freedom. It's been horrible. No, it hasn't! I realized, after it all, that I chose between having a baby and furthering my career. I chose the career because I knew how to do it and I didn't dare plunge into the awful abyss of motherhood. Who the hell gave women choices? It must have been so much easier just to have got pregnant and not be able to think about all this! *(laughter)*

HEATHER We spent so many years putting off having children, fending childbearing away, arguing for our right to get abortions, that it's almost impossible to change tracks now, don't you think? On the other hand, I still take it for granted that I do want to have children some day. It's in my head. But even if that's only fantasy, it keeps me happy for now.

GEORGINA Do you see a man around as the father? Or is it *you* and the child? People tell me that, with Martin, I didn't really want the man. I'm not so sure though.

HEATHER Ideally, I suppose I imagine I'll fall in love with someone with whom I'll want to share and have a child. But I haven't found that person yet. So I have to go on where I am now. I

157

have a few men I'm close to. I am looking for a man who would be a good father, someone who'd care. Not necessarily a man to live with me and the child, no.

GEORGINA Is it the nice, responsible but absentee father, who would live round the corner rather than in the tension of every-day sharing?

HEATHER We're all still in rooms of our own, aren't we?

GEORGINA What are we going to do about us all? Young guys seem to be in the same mess.

POLLY I seem to meet a lot of strong women and a lot of men who have suffered from the feminist movement. They're emasculated. I mean they've lost their sexuality, their raunchiness, their ability to turn us on. They're sweet enough.

HEATHER I always see it when I try and jive with them! On the dance floor the majority of guys our age let us do our own thing and make no attempt to lead us.

GEORGINA Oh God, what an image. Yes, I say 'You just stand there and I'll do my thing round you!' (*howls of laughter*)

ME And so we go on. Experimenting with life as we live it. Following roads, over uncharted territory, brave or scared by turns. Mostly we all agree we enjoy it. We reach out for life and want more of it. We want it to be hard and a challenge. As long as we're thinking, questioning, reaching out somewhere, we're happy. It's more rewarding to be like that than to be stuck in a rut with one set of ideas. But often it's hard and we shiver in fear. Oh well, as the song goes, 'For the spices of your life, You got to pay the price.' We chose to live this way. Here's looking at you, life.

John Nicholson
Habits 75p

'Each chapter deals with something most of us do, consciously or unconsciously, every day — living with other people and our surroundings, eating, remembering, winning and losing, believing, walking, smoking, pretending . . . jargon is kept to a minimum . . . the book is elegant and restrained' SPECTATOR

'Marvellous and riveting . . . readable and funny . . . comes up with some fascinating answers' Virginia Ironside WOMAN'S WORLD

Dr Richard Mackarness
Not All In The Mind 70p

In this new vitally important book, Dr Richard Mackarness, doctor and psychiatrist, shows how millions may be made ill, physically and mentally, by common foods such as milk, eggs, coffee and white flour.

He relates case after case from his clinical practice where patients with chronic ailments resistant to other methods of treatment were cured by identifying and eliminating foods to which they had developed unsuspected allergy.

Margaret Allen
The Money Book £1.75

Work out your income properly, fill in your tax return ; make the best use of your bank ; buy a freezer, a house or a car ; decide on an allowance for your children ; understand a company annual report ; make a will ; get a divorce ; invest in unit trusts or buy by mail order . . .

'The most comprehensive book about money' MANCHESTER EVENING NEWS

Frank Hardy
The Unlucky Australians £1.25

with an introduction by Gough Whitlam

A unique study of the Aboriginal Australian by one of Australia's
foremost writers, who set out into his country's landscape in
the tradition of Steinbeck's *Travels with Charley*. The outcome
of his journey is this powerful evocation of the modern Aborigine
and his world. To read it is to hear the voices – vivid and real – of
those Australians who have been shouldered aside – The Unlucky
Australians.

Stephen Vizinczey
In Praise of Older Women 80p

'A cool, comic survey of the sexual education of a young
Hungarian, from his first encounter, as a twelve-year-old refugee
with the American forces, to his unsatisfactory liaison with a
reporter's wife in Canada at 'the belated end of his youth', when
he was twenty-three . . . elegantly erotic, with masses of that
indefinable quality, style . . . this has the real stuff of immortality'
PUNCH

' . . . a writer of originality and grace . . . his novel is a delight'
GUARDIAN